Patterns of Settlement

Human Geography in Colour

D. C. Money, M.A., F.R.G.S.
Head of Geography Department, Bedford School

 Evans

Evans Brothers Limited London

Published by Evans Brothers Limited
Montague House, Russell Square, London, W.C.1

Evans Brothers (Nigerian Publishers) Limited
P.M.B. 5164, Ibadan, Nigeria

© D. C. Money 1972

Also by D. C. Money
The Earth's Surface
Physical Geography in Colour

Printed in Great Britain by W. S. Cowell Limited, Ipswich

SBN 237 28994 6 (limp)
SBN 237 28979 2 (cased)

Contents

Introduction

The interactions between man and his environment are complex and always changing. His very presence and the actions he takes in order to survive bring about such changes; and the actions themselves are usually strongly influenced by environmental conditions. They are not always logical responses, for man may act in a wayward manner, but on the whole they tend to create recognisable patterns of occupation.

Here we examine some of these locational patterns created by various groups of men, some living in simple rural communities strongly attached to the soil, occupying tiny hamlets or nucleated villages, others in modern urban complexes whose patterns and forms of growth are sometimes subject to rigorous planning, sometimes uncontrolled sprawls or obsolescent, deteriorating, residential relics.

In each location, the geographer aims to discover a certain order and to recognise patterns of human activity. In recent times his visual studies and verbal descriptions have been backed by more precise and objective methods of measurement and analysis. The geographer has begun to acquire quantified data, by field survey or from documentary sources, and to use new techniques for processing and presenting it.

There are many relatively straightforward ways in which this data may be statistically processed and analyses presented. Books are now available which demonstrate such techniques to students at various educational levels. This is a great step forward. There is a danger, however, that teachers and pupils alike come to look on the acquisition of such techniques as an end in itself, that they quantify for the sake of it, and in so doing lose sight of the aims of geographical studies.

Geographers must still be prepared to observe and describe the various complexities of human activities, and of the environment, with the help of a fundamental store of factual knowledge about the physical conditions, and the racial, historical, and social background of the peoples concerned. They must, at least, be aware that all these facts interact in intricate ways. They may then use their quantitative techniques more wisely to isolate and describe the most significant influences. Despite the increasing ease of travel, many student geographers necessarily have a limited knowledge of the earth's surface and its peoples, and their practical work usually relates to fairly local conditions. A book concerned with human geography must aim to stimulate a wider interest in mankind rather than concentrate entirely on local applications.

This book deals with observable patterns of human settlement, and points to methods of simplification which may be used to discover order in the location of human activities. But it also enables the student geographer to study many diverse forms of rural and urban settlement *first* and consider the numerous inter-acting influences which affect both simple and complex communities—peasant farmers and commuting business men alike. Part I, therefore, deals with forms of settlement, and examines the nature of the physical, economic, historic and social factors which influence these very varied communities.

Part II considers patterns in settlement: patterns from the past; patterns being created and destroyed; and points to likely patterns of development. Models and simple statistical methods of presentation are used primarily to illustrate their value to geographical studies. The abundant use of visual material should in itself act as a corrective for those who might see models and quantification as ends in themselves. The detailed examination of two contrasting urban areas helps to give greater reality to the descriptions of the methods of analysing locational patterns given in the text.

Some emphasis is placed on the need to examine the structure of simple rural communities and their environmental conditions as well as those of urban areas. This is indeed a 'pendulum swing'; for, until recently, many facts of urban geography had not been treated in any depth by geography students. Now that Urban Studies are very much 'in', it is common to find that the modes of life of hundreds of millions of people living close to the soil are perfunctorily treated, or glossed over, in the understandable urge to acquire geographical techniques applicable to the students' local environment. This book aims to broaden the outlook by presenting material from world-wide sources and with a wide pictorial coverage; for the fundamental aims of geographical studies have not changed. Human geography should still consider 'man' in the broadest sense.

Each of the colour photographs has been taken by the author. Acknowledgement is due to Aerofilms Ltd for the photographs used for Figs. 23, 24, 56, 58, 86, 89, 102, 106, 107, 123, 125, 129, 131, 147, 149, 153, 156, 169, 170, 174, 177, 189, 190, 191, 192. All line illustrations were drawn by Cartographic Enterprises.

D.C.M.

Part I Forms of Settlement

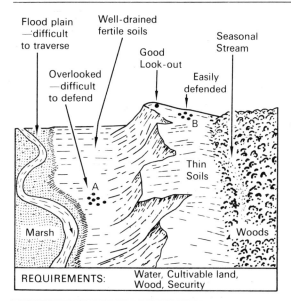

Flood plain —difficult to traverse

Well-drained fertile soils

Good Look-out

Seasonal Stream

Overlooked —difficult to defend

Easily defended

B

Thin Soils

A

Marsh

Woods

REQUIREMENTS: Water, Cultivable land, Wood, Security

Choice and Settlement

Fig. 1. Men could settle at A, near water and cultivable land, but it is insecure. B is easier to defend, closer to forest—though wood gathering is a periodic occupation. Perennial water is distant. Lowland soils could be cultivated and abandoned in time of trouble. Which combination of factors will most strongly influence a decision?—see p.64.

Fig. 2. East and West Kambalda, Western Australia (diagrammatic). The eastern town and treatment plant were quickly established near the first mine, to hasten production of nickel concentrate and so stimulate investment. The more exact positions of rich reserves were located later; these suggested that the town should not expand; so a western residential area was developed; a settlement pattern influenced by economic demands and time factors.

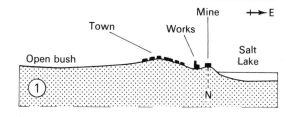

Town — Mine — Works — E

Open bush — Salt Lake

① N

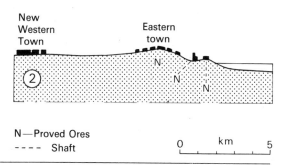

New Western Town — Eastern town

② N N N N

N—Proved Ores
---- Shaft

0 km 5

The Complexity of Human Settlement

Any systematic study of human settlement must be daunting, and for many reasons. There are thousands of millions of people, diverse in race, social habits, and economic assets. There are great differences between the mode of life of urban communities, many in great cities, and of millions of peasant peoples caught in seemingly inescapable rural poverty. The factors affecting their particular clusters of population, their forms of settlement, intercommunications, and modes of living are many and complex.

Whether the study is local or on a world scale, the geographer must be prepared to make his own assessment of the most crucial factors affecting the form, structure, growth, or decline of the settlement he investigates. But even with his essential training and experience, the interaction of these factors may be so involved that the use of modern aids, quantitative techniques, and perhaps computers, are needed

before he can make a realistic assessment of their relative importance.

Human Choice—Conflicting Factors

As we study an occupied landscape we may find various regularities in man's developments—some evidence of settlement patterns, or perhaps a hierarchy (regular grading) of urban centres. But any ideas of inevitability should be discontinued from the start; for an act of settlement involves choice, and man must weigh conflicting factors against each other before making his choice. Often he is not aware of all the snags or advantages; and sometimes his actions are wayward. Before a well-balanced form of settlement becomes established, trial and error may well play a part; even then the balance may be upset by fresh technological advances—such as the construction of a by-pass road or a new airport. Figs. 1 and 2 illustrate two contrasting instances

involving choice and chance. Fig. 1 shows a simple tribal group faced with decisions—whether to settle at A or B, or elsewhere: on p. 64 we see how one choice may appear to be the more logical.

Fig. 2 shows how remote economic considerations may be influential. To create confidence in investors, nickel concentrates must be produced, and a township is sited. Later, rich ores are proved beneath the original township; and so a new residential area is created, well clear: thus dual townships result from pressures and chance factors.

Knowing What to Look For

The first part of this book stresses influential factors affecting settlements, from the simple and transitory to the complex. The trained geographer should look at the human landscape with some understanding of the interacting factors which have created it; he may then use quantitative methods to reveal their relationships more precisely.

Semi-Nomadic Movements: Settlement and Territorial Occupation

Fig. 3. A Masai carrying spear and knobkerry strides across a low volcanic mound near Mt. Meru in northern Tanzania; his herd H grazes the savannah grassland. Beyond are the eroded ashy slopes of an old volcano V; notice how the volcanic ridges R support different grasses and deciduous bushes.

The Masai

The once-powerful semi-nomadic Masai occupy a restricted, but still large, territory on the East African tablelands. Their cattle are their wealth, and they have traditionally scorned a settled agricultural existence. Fig. 8 shows many of the inter-related influences on such a people and their way of life.

Semi-permanent manyattas act as well-organised bases. A high thorn fence around the manyatta protects them and their stock from wild animals. Each of the low huts has a framework of thin branches and is thatched with long dry grass; some are covered with hides, and each of them plastered with clay and dung. In the single room are cooking pots, gourds, wood and other possessions. Manyattas are established in regions with permanent water-holes, usually on those higher

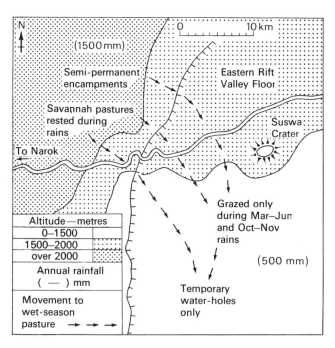

Fig. 5. Seasonal movements of Masai with herds into the Eastern Rift Valley of Kenya.

parts of the tablelands which have sufficient grazing to support cattle for long periods.

From these bases young men, with spear, short sword or knobkerry, and buffalo hide shield for protection, move their large herds slowly over the grasslands. As Fig. 5 shows, they move into the broad Eastern Rift Valley when the wetter periods bring fresh grazing there; this enables the higher pastures to be rested.

Milk, meat and blood form the diet of the young moran (warrior). The older men, and women and children, in the manyatta also possess varying numbers of sheep, goats and donkeys, and supplement their diet with flour, beans and potatoes, bought or exchanged for hides or meat. The site of the manyatta is changed from time to time, and a new base for the group is established.

Fig. 6. (above) *A Masai group with weapons. In this dry woodland savannah of southern Kenya, lions and leopards frequently menace the herds.*

Fig. 7. (below) *A temporary Masai manyatta, recently abandoned. The framework of the huts can be seen through the plastering.*

Chapter I
Temporary Settlement

Semi-Nomadism

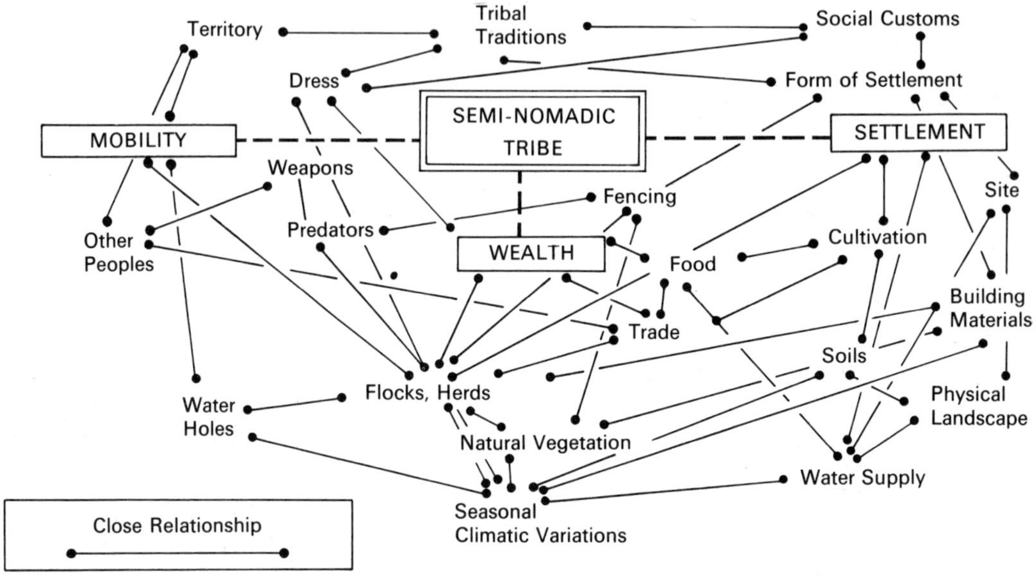

Fig. 8. The nature of movements, form of settlements, and social behaviour are affected by many inter-related factors. Here, those concerned with nomadic movement are shown on the left, those with settlement on the right; the tribal wealth depends on the type of nomadism and the character and extent of settlement.

Despite the increasing use of irrigation, spread of public works, and improvements in transport, millions of people still live a wandering or nomadic life. In this instance, settlement has no meaning except in the sense of acknowledged tribal boundaries and the necessity of following particular routes to water-holes or grazing land.

In parts of the Middle East and the Sahara, the Bedouin and other tribal groups still move with their camels, halting briefly at watering-points, or in wadis with a temporary supply of grazing. Theirs is a precarious existence; for apart from the harshness of climate and relief, freedom of movement is generally decreasing, and many are being persuaded to adopt simple forms of pastoralism.

Semi-Nomadic Practices

Simple forms of settlement are found among semi-nomadic tribes like the Turkhana, Somali, Rendille, and Boran herdsmen of the Kenya-Somali border-lands. The seasonal variations of climate and vegetation in a semi-arid environment are the chief influences on their way of life. Summer rains may consist of a few downpours only, but over several weeks sufficient vegetation will grow to support grazing animals on the move. Cattle are their real wealth, but camels, which also supply meat and milk, and donkeys carry household necessities and framework for temporary dwellings. Goats and sheep are other sources of meat, milk and skins. The various animals may be taken to pastures of different quality, and a family may therefore split up as they seek grazing.

In some places there are small areas of better soil, likely to remain moist for a while during the summer rains. One of these may act as a temporary base for the family group, who may return there each year to plant millet. The yield is small, but any extra food is valuable in a harsh environment.

Many parts of the African tablelands have thin sandy soils formed on old crystalline rocks, or lateritic soils with a shallow hardpan. Such soils are generally unsuitable for cultivation, but support a savannah grassland-with-trees suitable for grazing, provided the animals are kept on the move. In places, alluvial deposits or fertile volcanic soils may allow cultivation. Here settlement may be virtually permanent; though the family may again be divided during the year as the young men move their cattle over the grasslands, leaving the older men and women to grow food crops.

Their cultivation is often of a shifting type, and peoples like the Masai abandon their temporary homesteads from time to time and move to a new base, about which their animals may graze when the wandering herdsmen return during the local rainy seasons (p. 3).

Inter-relationships

The use of models, as in Figs. 8 and 9, make us aware that there are many interacting factors affecting even simple forms of settlement.

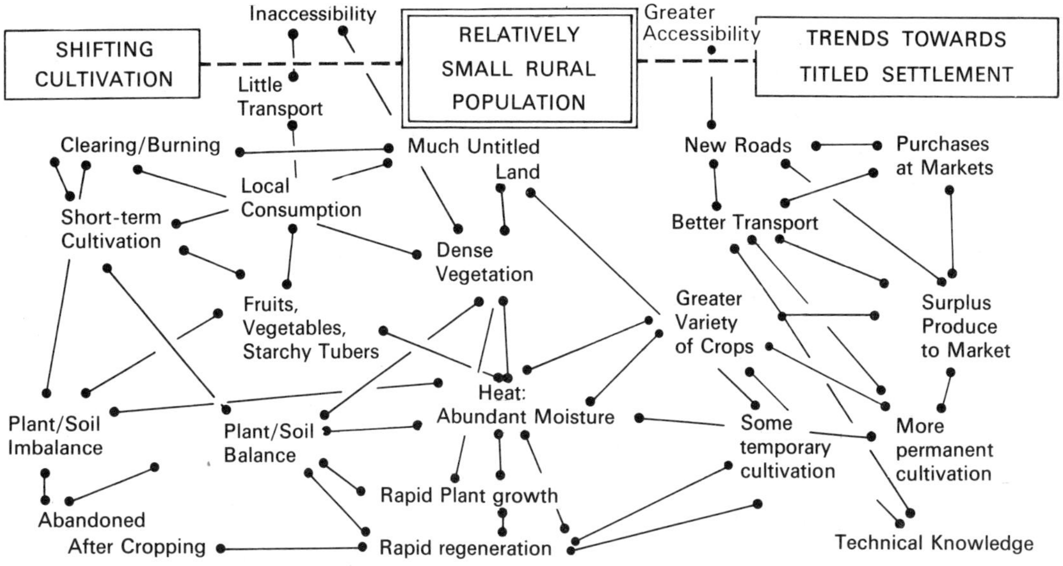

Fig. 9. The density of rural population is low, and, under certain climatic/vegetational conditions, people may support themselves by shifting cultivation in harmony with their environment, as indicated to the left. Other factors (right) are involved in movements towards titled land-holdings.

In some places one factor may have a dominant influence, while others are of negligible importance. It is possible to combine 'weightings', allotted to factors known to exert a particular influence, with a simple model, like that on p. 64, in order to examine the likely activities of a particular group in a specific environment.

Fig. 8 shows that semi-nomadic peoples usually have three main sources of food—direct from their animals, from cultivation, and from sale or exchange of animal commodities; hides may also be exchanged for cloth, dyes, oil, or other simple possessions.

Seasonal climatic variations affect the grazing, planting of crops, water supply, and paths of movement in times of drought or flood. Soils, themselves affected by climatic features, may suit or discourage close settlement. The presence or absence of predators, which menace the herds, depends partly on climatic/vegetational conditions; responses to these are seen in the weapons carried and in the fencing needed about cattle enclosures.

Contacts with other peoples and the acquisition of technical skills must, of course, affect the semi-nomadic way of life; and customs and traditions, as well as natural conditions, influence dress, forms of settlement and territorial bounds.

Shifting Cultivation

In many hot, relatively moist regions, where the vegetation cover is close and regenerates rapidly, men clear the land of rainforest, woodland, or woodland-savannah for temporary cultivation; but abandon it after a few years when the soil fertility begins to be exhausted.

Bushes are slashed away, branches cut, and the whole area burnt over. Ashes temporarily enrich soils in the spaces cleared amid the charred stumps. The practice is often termed 'slash-and-burn'. A variety of plants is then grown in the small patches, usually with the help of a light hoe, and the land may yield several crops a year.

Several years' repeated cropping depletes the soils; and exposure to heavy rainfall, with periods of strong, drying sun under tropical conditions, may lead to erosion unless a vegetation cover is re-established. So the plots are then abandoned and revert to secondary growth, perhaps a scrub-woodland or bushy savannah. The cultivators move on and clear elsewhere. Settlement under these conditions is again of a temporary nature. Housing and storages are of simple local materials.

However, in time, other factors may lead to more permanent settlement within the territorial limits of the group of cultivators. Tracks may come to be used as recognised trade routes and become incentives for settlement as dwellings concentrate along the line of the 'road'. A type of agriculture involving some kind of land rotation may then evolve, eventually leading to more permanent settlement.

This form of agriculture can be found in the Congo Basin, the tropics of South and Central America, and many parts of south-east Asia (p. 6).

Shifting Cultivation

Fig. 10. An area amid forest in southern Ceylon which has been cleared for temporary cultivation. Only small patches of cleared land are cultivated ; here cassava and vegetables are growing in crudely fenced, or marked, plots. Notice the burnt tree trunk (right), and secondary bush covering once-cultivated land (to the far right).

Chena Cultivation in Ceylon

In southern Ceylon there is a zone somewhat drier than the rice-growing alluvial coastlands of the south-west, though much of it bears forest and close woodland-savannah; it is still sparsely populated. Here a form of shifting cultivation (*chena*) is practised. An area of close vegetation is cleared by slash-and-burn methods and small parcels of land are cultivated by groups of people working jointly, sharing the maize, millet, vegetables, and chillies they produce. After several croppings—sometimes after a single cropping—they abandon the patches and move on to clear land not recently cultivated, where secondary plant growth has helped regenerate soil fertility. After a lengthy period they may return to clear the original patches once again.

They build temporary houses of branches and straw, with small thatched huts on poles as look-outs, for there are many wild animals in this part of the country.

In these districts there are, in fact, many settlement forms. Some chena cultivators plant a cash crop; while peasants live near the few main roads in small permanent settlements, some using irrigation for growing rice and fruits. The latter may also practice chena cultivation in nearby woodland, and if their clearing is far from the permanent small-holdings on which most of the cash crops are grown, some of their family group may still live in temporary housing.

Pure chena cultivation for subsistence is still found far from the through roads. The roads themselves stimulate commerce and the growth of cash crops, for sale by the roadside or at markets, like Wellawaya. Increasing population is also tending to break down the simpler forms of slash-and-burn subsistence economy, though this is still a common practice.

Fig. 11. Small-holdings like this are established alongside the road from Wellawaya market to the coast of southern Ceylon. The house, of local materials, stands amid cassava bushes, pawpaws and bananas; behind the house the family grows maize, vegetables, and gourds, like the one carried by the woman in the foreground. Immediately beyond their holding the land is cultivated on a shifting basis.

Transhumance

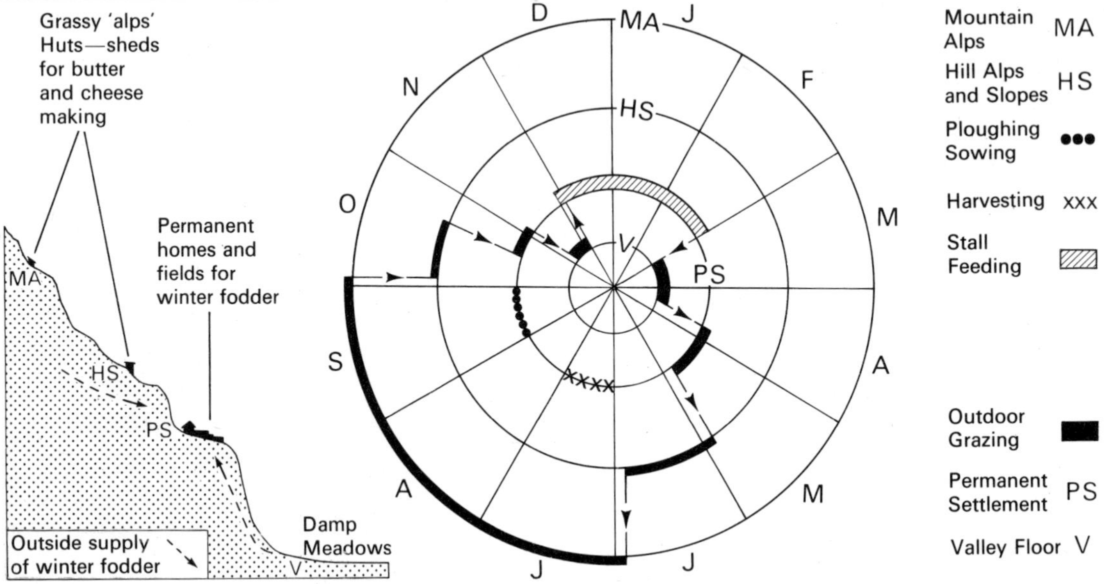

Grassy 'alps'
Huts—sheds for butter and cheese making

Permanent homes and fields for winter fodder

MA

HS

PS

Outside supply of winter fodder

Damp Meadows

V

Legend:
- Mountain Alps — MA
- Hill Alps and Slopes — HS
- Ploughing Sowing — ●●●
- Harvesting — xxx
- Stall Feeding — ▨
- Outdoor Grazing — ▬
- Permanent Settlement — PS
- Valley Floor — V

Fig. 12. The monthly chart shows typical activities during the year in the Alpine environment shown diagrammatically in the section, relating to each of the vertical zones—V, PS, HS, MA. Notice the short spring and late-autumn descents to the valley floor, and the varied activities in the zone of permanent settlement.

Types of Transhumance

The seasonal movements of animals from grazing, or stall-feeding, in the vicinity of permanent rural settlements to distant pastures is known as *transhumance*. In temperate lands this often means vertical movements from winter quarters in farms on hillsides, or valley floors, to summer pastures in the mountains, as practised in Switzerland and Scandinavia. Sometimes this involves long-distance droving; as in the movements of sheep from the Spanish meseta to the Pyrenees.

Norwegian Fiord Farming

Along the Norwegian fiords, occasional marine terraces, or higher breaks of slope, provide sufficient space for small farms. In the spring the livestock moves up fiordside paths to pastures on the high fjeld. They graze common land, shared by families who each have a small saeter, or log cabin, for their herders, with a cowshed and hut for cheese- and butter-making.

Although children may be taken up during the summer, most of the family remains below, where hay, root crops, oats for winter fodder, and vegetables are cultivated. The animals are brought down in early autumn, and remain in the barn, supplied with fodder, for much of the winter.

Alpine Dairy Farming

In the Swiss and French Alps the herds usually go to the high pastures in early June and stay until the end of September, travelling many kilometres from the village. Sheep may accompany them, and pastures are so allocated that dairy animals have the best grazing and sheep the higher, more rocky parts.

Again, only a few men temporarily occupy the mountain chalets, moving the animals from one grassy alp to another, and making butter and cheese. Fodder crops are grown about the permanent homes.

The actual movements may be complex, and Fig. 12 summarises month-by-month activities between Alpine valleys and high alps, where several stages of vertical movement are involved, above and below the settlement, each designed to make the most of outdoor grazing.

Other Seasonal Movements to Pastures

In the Mediterranean lands transhumance has been widespread, with sheep moving long distances—seen, particularly, in movements from summer pastures in the high Abruzzi of central Italy to lower, milder, grazing in Apulia during winter; though continued enclosure of common land and afforestation is curtailing these movements. Sometimes there is inverse transhumance from high settlements, as in parts of the Pyrenees where the slopes become too dry in summer, and stock is moved *down* to the steppes of Aragon. Transhumance is practised in many other parts of the world.

Chapter II
Permanent Rural Settlement

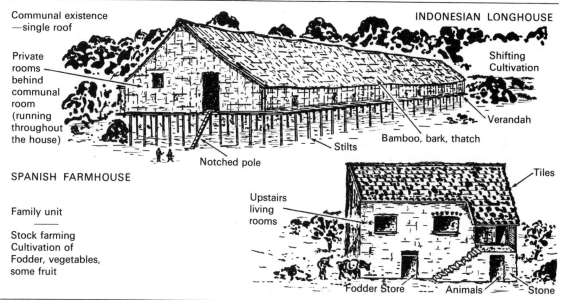

INDONESIAN LONGHOUSE

Communal existence —single roof

Private rooms behind communal room (running throughout the house)

Shifting Cultivation

Verandah

Stilts

Bamboo, bark, thatch

Notched pole

SPANISH FARMHOUSE

Tiles

Upstairs living rooms

Family unit

Stock farming
Cultivation of
Fodder, vegetables,
some fruit

Fodder Store

Animals

Stone

Fig. 13. The few examples shown here, and in Fig. 17, illustrate how natural features and human activities combine to influence the size, shape, ground-plan and materials used in rural dwellings. The social customs of a communal group or isolated family, the collective cultivation or small-scale pastoralism, and the availability of local materials are reflected in the forms of the Indonesian longhouse and Spanish mountain farmhouse.

Land Tenure

From nomadic movements with animals and forms of shifting cultivation, men have come to establish and maintain permanent pastures and to cultivate pieces of land marked out, and established in law, as a 'holding'.

Other activities immediately stem from this: the creation of permanent dwellings, regular water supplies, the maintenance of communications with neighbours, and steps to protect possessions.

The extension of land-holdings, and the development of new forms of cultivation, create, in time, changing patterns of land-use about individual farms or hamlets. Page 72 examines some of the land-use patterns which may evolve about simple settlements.

The buildings on each holding vary with their function—dwelling, store, fortification—and their form depends on other human and regional characteristics. Obviously their nature varies greatly from one part of the world to another; variety in materials

used, and in plan and structure, are seen in many of the photographs in the book.

The Evolution of Rural Dwellings

In any settled region *time*, an important factor in all human studies, brings changes in the form of buildings. As time passes, men acquire knowledge and develop new techniques. But the rate of technical-cultural advancements differs from one region to another. 'Stone Age' dwellings do not necessarily belong to the remote past. Just as nomadic life exists in some areas as it has done for thousands of years, so the use of stone implements persists—as in parts of New Guinea, where technology is on a level with that developed in north-west Europe thousands of years ago. And so with buildings; in some parts of the Mediterranean lands, rural dwellings have changed little in form and function from the days of earliest settlement.

Social and Economic Factors

The type of materials and method of construction employed in building depend not only on the local climate, structure and topography, but also on the social and economic status of the occupants. In the moist tropics, the crude pole-and-palm-thatch one-room structure of a labouring family, or poor tenant farmer, contrasts with the spacious, elaborately decorated building of the land-owner, even though the materials used may be broadly similar. Varying social habits and requirements, the need for an office, library, place of entertainment or display, all make for obvious differences in size and form of construction.

The transport of materials is usually costly, so the labourer, or tenant farmer, tends to make do with local supplies, whereas a richer family may import materials from afar, and also use the decorative skill of architects from outside the community (Figs. 15 and 16).

Rural Homestead

The form of this Jamaican house, the materials with which it is built, and the actual location of the small-holding, are all influenced by a combination of physical, climatic, and economic factors. The small dwelling on a narrow river terrace is constructed of timber and roofed with corrugated iron—the often unsightly, but cheap and effective roofing in lands of heavy tropical rainfall. The lean-to is of local materials, thatched with palm fronds.

There are numerous small-holdings of this type on land unprofitable for estate farming. For in a hot moist climate, where natural vegetation and cultivated plants grow profusely, a family may be relatively poor but able to grow a variety of food and cash crops. Here, besides vegetables, cultivated among the trees to the right, are coffee bushes, citrus trees, bananas, and coconut palms, in a tangle of productive vegetation.

A road runs down-valley, and, not far off, is a junction served by public transport, used for school journeys and visits to a market centre and coastal town. This is the smallest unit in the hierarchy of settlements ranging from isolated farms and small hamlets, through village settlements, to towns and cities. The work is done by members of the family, and embellishments to the house itself are limited by a low income.

Fig. 14. House and lean-to on a small-holding in the Buff Bay river valley, in north-eastern Jamaica.

Rural settlement is seldom composed of dwellings belonging to people of similar social status or with equal incomes. Also there is often a marked difference between the poorer rural dwellers who have their own small-holdings and those who must seek employment, and a wage, to ensure subsistence.

The family house of the small-holder in Fig. 14 contrasts with those of the poor in Fig. 16, who, in an over-populated region, have only unskilled or semi-skilled labour to offer. In this group, the central home was that of the original small-holder; the others have had to be built of wood gleaned, or obtained cheaply.

In contrast, Fig. 15 shows a house which was built in European style, modified to suit tropical colonial conditions, in a district of Kingston which was once a sugar estate, but has become part of the outer suburbs of high-quality dwellings. These are striking contrasts, but not untypical of rural countrysides the world over: so often the large farmhouse, with style and ornamentation reflecting a period of prosperous agriculture, is neighbour to the small tied cottages of farm workers. In other words, the characteristics of rural dwellings, while responding to local physical conditions, also reflect social and economic ones.

Fig. 15. (above) *A mansion of the mid-colonial period, now in the outer suburbs of Kingston, Jamaica.*

Fig. 16. (below) *Poor housing in the countryside some kilometres beyond the outskirts of Kingston.*

Rural Dwellings

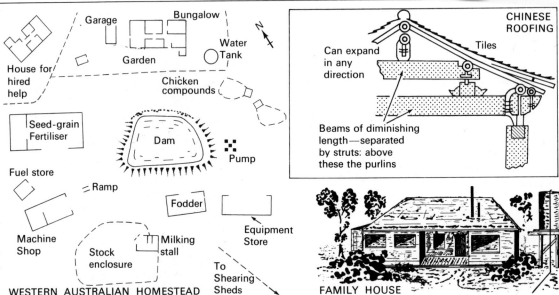

Fig. 17. *The lay-out of homestead and farm buildings near Bencubbin, Western Australia (Fig. 136). The mechanical equipment needed to farm thousands of hectares with little, if any, help outside the family, must be housed and maintained. Fodder is stored; but wheat and wool are despatched to temporary storages near the railway, some 15 km away.*

The inset *shows how the Chinese beam frame technique allows more flexible roof styles than the rigid Western triangulated trusses.*

Local Influences and Modern Trends

The use of local materials is still apparent in Britain: flints in the walls of East Anglian houses, alongside others with characteristic weather-boarding; grey grit-stones in Pennine villages; and red sandstone blocks of Exmoor farms, with boundary walls of local shales.

Climatic influences are usually apparent, as we can see in the flat-topped roofs of Karmi (Fig. 26), the tall, cool shuttered rooms of Casares in southern Spain (Fig. 56), and the steep-pitched slate roofs in the wetter climatic region of the valleys of South Wales (Fig. 67).

But with the mass-production of materials and improvements in transport, local influences are bound to be less obvious. The widespread use of corrugated-iron roofing in tropical settlements illustrates this only too well—ugly but functional. Easily transportable sectional housing allows new settlements to be developed in universal styles and built from materials made in distant lands.

However, strong climatic influences are still evident in the form of some modern dwellings. Newly built rural houses amid the farmlands of the St. Lawrence Valley in Canada have a bungalow appearance above ground, but incorporate a floor almost below ground-level, lit by low half-windows; this is occupied mainly during the bitterly cold winter, and used for storage space in the hot summer months.

Cultural and Traditional Influences

Regional styles of decoration may be transferred by colonisation. Typical Dutch gabling is seen in Boer farmhouses in South Africa.

Sometimes the styles are due to technical developments which are in common regional use. In China the use of the beam-frame system (Fig. 17) enables the roof to expand in any direction; interlocking tiling allows gentle gradations, resulting in the sweeping curves so typical of houses in China and the adjacent parts of eastern Asia, and in contrast to the Western roofs of triangle-and-truss structure.

Elsewhere, as Fig. 13 shows, social factors influence the form of dwelling: the Borneo Dyaks live a communal existence in the security of their raised longhouse, with each family looking after a cross-section of the building—their private room, and part of the long communal room and outer verandah, both of which run through the house.

Economic Functions and Lay-Out

Above all, the economic functions have a great influence on the lay-out of the farm unit. Fig. 17 shows the variety of buildings needed to enable the large wheat and sheep farm in this dry, inner part of agricultural Western Australia to function efficiently. Compare this with the combined animal/family living unit seen in Fig. 13.

Small Nucleated Settlements

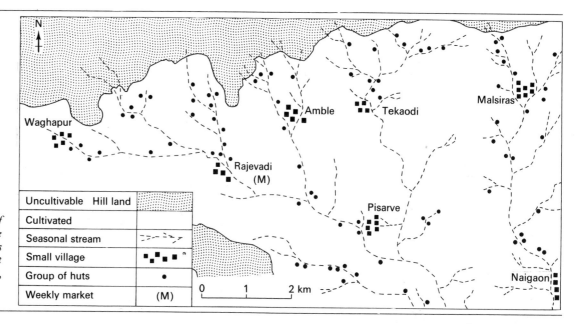

Fig. 18. Cultivated land on the Indian Deccan, east of Poona, where settlement is clustered about wells along the seasonal streams. Small villages connected by cart-tracks lie 3–4 km apart. Weekly markets in this district are at centres 20 km apart—Rajevadi (Thurs.), Sasvad (Mon.), and Jejuri (Sun.).

Uncultivable Hill land	
Cultivated	
Seasonal stream	
Small village	
Group of huts	
Weekly market	(M)

Small Compact Settlements

In some parts of the world, small market towns serve farmers who mostly live in dispersed houses amid their own agricultural land. This is the usual settlement-form of small-holders in the densely populated Baganda and Busoga districts north of Lake Victoria (pp. 22–23). In the English countryside, large farms commonly stand amid their enclosed fields, and, in central North America, farms with their outhouses, stores, and workshops are dispersed across the rectangularly patterned landscape. (Fig. 123). However, until the nineteenth century most people in northern Europe lived in small clustered rural settlements; and today in many parts of southern Europe and Asia the houses of farmers and rural craftsmen are grouped together amid the cultivated landscape.

Compact nucleated settlements have generally begun as family units, or inter-related groups or clans, living together in small agricultural communities in order to tackle various tasks communally, and to make best use of their craftsmen.

Certain physical conditions have favoured rural nucleation. In a dry climate, or on permeable rocks with a low water-table, initial settlement would tend to concentrate near surface water, if any, or about a well; whereas plentiful surface water would allow dispersal, but would not necessarily determine this. Simple settlement would avoid poorly-drained land and concentrate on areas of well-drained, easily worked soils; in which case a limited area of cultivable land would encourage nucleation, leaving as much of the land as possible for agriculture. Fig 23 shows how limited cultivable land is divided into individual strips, farmed from a nucleated settlement. Near York, in eastern England, most lowland villages are on sandy soils, unfavourable for arable farming but adjacent to more fertile, heavier, clay soils which are closely cultivated.

Particular sites may also favour grouping, and low flood-free terraces, with access to land workable when drained, have been favoured sites throughout the English midlands. Water, as a negative influence, has also often led to settlement concentration near a ford or bridgehead.

The Spread of Settlement

As men colonised large potentially fertile areas, during the Anglo-Saxon occupation of the British lowlands for instance, each nucleated group acquired enough land to grow grain, graze cattle, and supply wood sufficient to support the whole community. Eventually, with natural increase and new arrivals, there would be insufficient land within easy reach of the nucleus. So that some moved out, to clear and settle new land; and, in turn, this secondary settlement eventually hived off other settlers.

Such expansion from 'founder' villages has occurred in many lowland areas—on the Indo-Gangetic Plain and in the Sudan, for instance. But, outside economic influences can quickly change the pattern of early colonisation, (see p. 20).

Farm Units and Small Hamlets

These large farms and adjoining hamlets in the Derbyshire Pennines and West-country vale stand amid enclosed fields in a countryside of peaceful security; though it is not unusual in Britain to see old fortified manor houses and farms, some of them moated (Fig. 129)—though perhaps for drainage as much as for defence.

Each of these units is in a pastoral landscape, a cluster of buildings with different functions—residence, milking sheds, barns for storage and a lean-to where farm machinery may be housed and maintained. Before the days of mechanisation, this type of enclosed farming had become typical of Britain, contrasting with communal open-field farming and the small holdings of peasant cultivation.

Regional characteristics are seen in the buildings and enclosures. The mountain limestone of the buildings, and stone walls blend with exposures in the dry valleys and through relatively thin soils of this Derbyshire landscape (see also Fig. 24). The hard sandstones of high Exmoor overlook the fertile Vale of Porlock, with deep soils suitable for fodder crops as well as high-quality sown pastures for dairy stock; the steeper slopes carry many sheep. Here the buildings are of Old Red Sandstone.

Most of the labourers live close to their place of work, though today, with improved transport, some come from a distance. Their groups of cottages and farm buildings make up the small hamlets, like Tivington, where the tiny church and dwellings are the only functional units—since Porlock and Minehead, some 4–5 km away, provide most of the goods and services needed. In the same way, Buxton, rather than the neighbouring village, serves the Pennine hamlet.

Fig. 19. (above) *A large stock farm on the Derbyshire Pennines, south-east of Buxton. Notice the dry valley, limestone outcrops and dry stone walls.*

Fig. 20. (below) *A dairy farm near the small hamlet of Tivington in the Vale of Porlock, West Somerset. Beyond, the plateau of Exmoor overlooks the Bristol Channel.*

Clustered Settlement on a Defensive Site

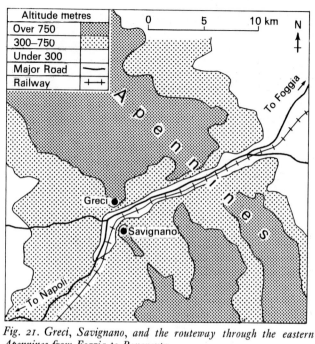

Fig. 21. *Greci, Savignano, and the routeway through the eastern Apennines from Foggia to Benevento.*

Hill-top sites in southern Italy are often occupied by nucleated villages, which have taken advantage of a defensive position, even though it has meant long daily journeys to surrounding cultivable land. In many parts of southern and eastern Europe such a village has grown to become an 'agrotown'—a large nucleated settlement still closely related to the agricultural countryside, with many men and women travelling daily to work in the adjacent fields; see also Fig. 60.

Here Savignano, and its 'twin' town, Greci, to the north, occupy particularly strong strategic positions, overlooking a major routeway through the eastern Apennines. Their functions remain predominantly rural, with small fields of vegetables and fruit trees about the towns, pasture and wheatgrowing on the lower slopes, and much rough grazing on the steeper hillsides.

Fig. 22. *The hill settlement of Savignano, occupying a saddle on the southern side of the gap (left) through the Apennines. Notice the tight cluster of housing, and the open countryside about the town.*

15

Nucleated Village and Strip Cultivation

Fig. 23. In Switzerland the cultivation of scattered strips on unenclosed land has been common practice about nucleated villages on the plateau lands of ancient settlement. Here, arable land amid the forest about Aarwanger is divided into numerous small, fragmented holdings.

Since World War II, much of this fragmented land has been regrouped to form large compact holdings, accessible by new roads in some cases; sometimes with new farms within the larger holdings.

Compact Village in a Dry Landscape

Fig. 24. Foolow, on the dry Pennine limestone uplands, east of Buxton in Derbyshire, is a compact settlement, its buildings clustered about the green and pond.

Stone-walls enclose the fields of a stock-farming countryside which lacks surface water; notice the lines of sink-holes, solution hollows, and dry valleys.

Relief and Dispersal

Throughout the Blue Mountains of Jamaica the physical conditions have both beneficial and adverse effects on rural settlement. Heat and moisture through the year favour rapid plant growth, especially in areas where potentially fertile soils are developed on the mixed debris of the more gentle slopes. But heavy rainfall causes slips and slumps on the more unstable slopes, and extends gullies headwards. Farms tend only to occupy the former, and so are dispersed and small. Communications are difficult in such rugged country.

The population pressures and the overall economy of this relatively small island affect settlement within the mountains. Many parts of Jamaica are over-populated, and much land is taken up by sugar estates. There is poverty in the overcrowded central areas of Kingston, and about its fringes, and there is limited employment. In the mountains small-holders can make a living, and perhaps sell surplus produce from settlements of the type seen in Fig. 14. Because of the scale of the country, Kingston's markets are not far away and lorries follow well-developed north-south routes through the mountains. Lateral communications are difficult, yet low land values allow a few farms to be established where there is sufficient cultivable land. As well as growing bananas and coffee, they produce vegetables for town markets. In places, nurseries grow young trees for planting on the hillsides to check erosion.

Fig. 25. A farm on a Blue Mountain spur, whose sides are terraced and planted with conifers. Bananas and coffee are grown on the hillsides, and some of the terraces planted as tree nurseries. Above new terracing, yellow plastic sheeting covers young plants. The isolation is emphasised by the winding road hugging the hillsides, connecting the farm with the Kingston-Buff Bay road. High humidity produces the haze which gives the mountains their name.

Fig. 26. Karmi, like other villages on the seaward side of the mountains of northern Cyprus, developed as a clustered settlement where springs issue from limestone rocks, though water is now piped to the village. Agricultural land-use shows zoning about the settlement (Fig. 100). This is partly because the water accessibility varies with distance and partly because labour-demanding crops tend to occupy land near the centre of settlement (p. 72). So there are fruits and vegetables on scree slopes close to the village and pastures beneath the olives further off (foreground), away from the main water sources; but nearer the coast mechanical pumps now irrigate citrus groves.

Small Rural Settlements

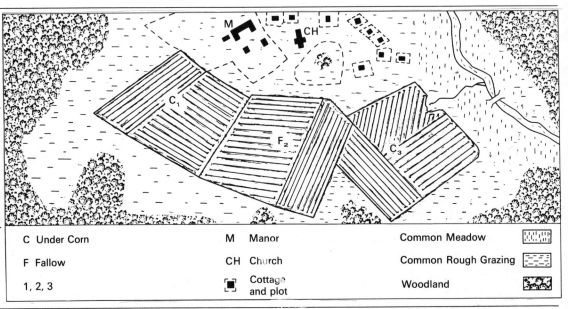

Fig. 27. A diagrammatic lay-out of a village community in Medieval Britain, with a three-field system adjusted to relief and drainage, allowing two fields to be cropped and one fallow each year. Peasants cultivated plots about hovels, or cottages of local materials. They worked individual scattered strips in the main fields. They contributed produce to the manor and tended land about the manor house and out-buildings. The latter, with the church, are of more durable structure and materials. The ridges and furrows created by strip-ploughing are still apparent in enclosed fields of the English midlands, and in some places the whole pattern of the three-field system may be seen beneath present-day pastures (Fig. 57). Some villages disappeared with en-closures, but many remain as the basic units of rural settle-ment in the English countryside.

C	Under Corn	M	Manor	Common Meadow
F	Fallow	CH	Church	Common Rough Grazing
1, 2, 3		▣	Cottage and plot	Woodland

Rural Colonisation and Land-Use

In areas of peasant farming, in southern Asia and Central America for example, the nature, optimum size, and number of rural settlements in a fertile region depend on agricultural organisation as well as population increase. This was the case in Medieval Britain, which inherited a feudal open-field system.

In such a system, the nucleated village was a compact centre of activity, with men working for a common good, whatever their additional dues might be—an optimum settlement form, which minimised the movements of men and animals. Sometimes, however, as the population grew, fields were extended, so that field labour had to travel far from the village; the consequent establishment of new settle-ment can be seen in England, and other lands with comparable systems, where the parent settlement has bequeathed its name to a later one, sometimes with the pre-fix 'new', 'lower', or 'higher'.

Outside Influences and Dispersal

At times, economic circumstances created by national policies or land-owner's dictates, cause changes beyond the villagers' control. During the 15th and 16th centuries, English landlords converted many open arable fields to large, hedged enclosures for pasturing sheep and cattle—an economy needing few men. Open-field strips disappeared under grass; and, as people migrated, many villages were abandoned; scattered, isolated large farms became a feature of the landscape. Further enclosures took place during the 18th and 19th centuries, causing rural migration, though not the overall abandonment of settlements of the earlier period.

Such disintegration of nucleated settlements has not been confined to Britain. In Denmark and Sweden, from the 18th century, many nucleated villages have given place to scattered farms estab-lished in the fields. In many parts of Western Europe men have farmed fragmented strips about villages until quite recently (Fig. 23), but the last thirty years has seen much consolidation and re-allocation of uneconomical fragments, and, in some cases, movements from village nuclei to new farm settle-ments.

An irregular scatter of farms and small hamlets, amidst cultivated land, is apt to occur in upland country of strong relief (and on lowlands where there are not the factors of constraint which lead to nucleation). Small hamlets and isolated farms are common in the more remote parts of western Scot-land, Exmoor, Brittany, and the Ardennes, where land-use has long been mainly pastoral, employing relatively few people.

Pioneer Settlement

Colonists from Western Europe, of many nations, have pioneered as individuals rather than groups.

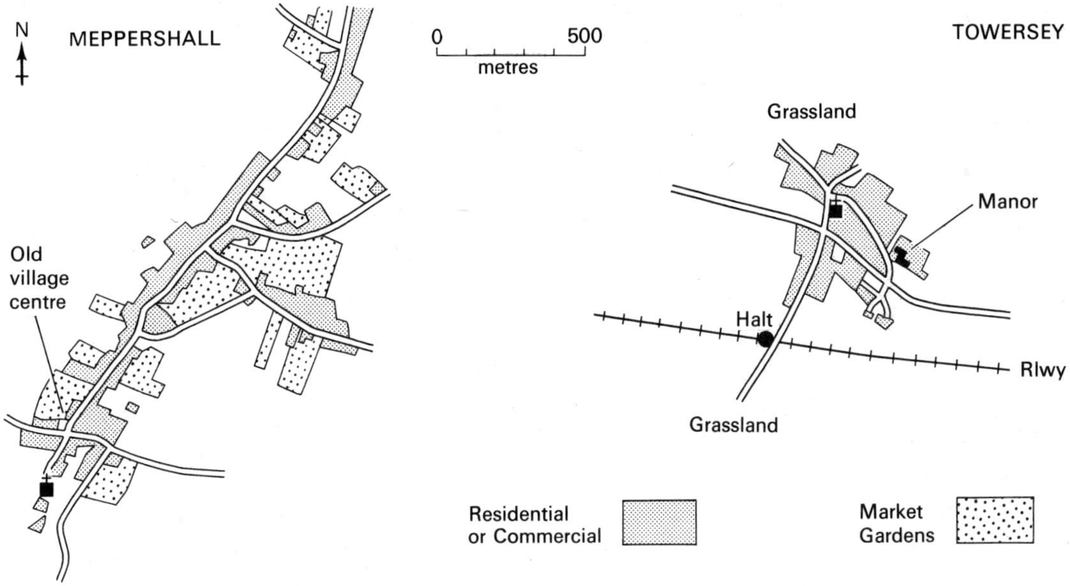

N MEPPERSHALL

0   500
metres

Grassland

Old
village
centre

Manor

Halt

Grassland

Rlwy

Residential
or Commercial

Market
Gardens

Fig. 28. Village forms are often connected with functions, and so may vary with time. Meppershall, in south Bedfordshire, was once a limited cluster of buildings about a crossroads near the church. With the development of market-gardening and recent residential increase, it has spread out along the roads, mainly to the north.

Towersey, near Thame, is set in a dairy-farming countryside. Most of its houses still cluster close to the old village nucleus, church, and manor house, though part of the population commutes to non-agricultural work.

In lowlands with much cultivable land and adequate water, an early colonist has freedom to choose and develop a site, if he has technical ability, capital and peaceful conditions. Thus the colonisation of plain-lands in North America and Australia saw individual homesteads develop, first in pioneer country, later on regularly distributed land units, so creating an areal grid pattern of properties and communications (p. 94). Service settlements became spaced fairly regularly across the landscape (p. 100), usually about cross-roads. The extent of such settlement was influenced by the routes of pioneer roads and railways, and, locally, by variations in relief, soil quality, and water resources.

Village Form and Function

In recently colonised lands, the grid pattern is the typical lay-out of service townships. But in countries of older settlement, villages have a variety of forms. Stress was once placed on relationships between ethnic groups of colonists and their settlement patterns and shapes of villages—isolated farmsteads of Celtic folk, compact settlements of Germanic peoples, and the creation of round- or street-villages by Slavs. In certain circumstances there were obvious correlations—many Celtic settlements *were* dispersed in rugged western highlands. But, there are many reasons why a village has a 'round' form. It may be an optimum form for efficient cultivation, as in small strongly nucleated settlements on the Indian Deccan (p. 13)—or, like so many Polish villages, it may have developed behind a ring-fence and retained its form. Again there are many linear road-villages. In the English midlands narrow holdings often lie at right angles to the road, with their houses on the roadside, an arrangement which preserves land from interference by minor routeways; many 'street-villages' of the Netherlands developed in the Middle Ages, as houses were sited along the banks of a dyke, their holdings stretching across drained land to the marshy fen. In eastern Canada,

French seigneuries were divided into long strips stretching back from the St. Lawrence, the farm houses a little way back, linked by a road parallel to the river. Today they form street-villages, focused at intervals on a church and stores.

With so many village types associated with each ethnic and national group, it is preferable to view the development of each settlement in its particular environment as a unique process.

Common advantages of site have led to such classifications as 'ford' or 'terrace' villages. There may have been strong locational influences, but it is preferable to study rural places in terms of their particular social and economic circumstances, and not place too much influence on genetic facts. This may well reveal relationships between the functions of a place, its size and its form.

Settlement Distribution – Small-holdings

Fig. 29. A family homestead in southern Uganda. The thatched roof, supported by strong poles, covers the circular house. The walls are of cane framework, with a plaster surface. Cassava and bananas grow to the right of the house. This narrow holding extends back for a hundred metres or so from the road.

The plateau of southern Uganda, north of Lake Victoria, is a landscape of flat-topped hills, whose lateritic capping supports poor bush savannah. It is cut by valleys, whose floors may contain papyrus swamp. However, the gentle slopes between hill-top and valley bottom have deeper, mixed soils, formed under rainforest, natural to conditions of high humidity and mean monthly temperatures above 20°C.

Most people live on the middle slopes, or gentle ridges between valleys. Very few live in villages, but occupy small-holdings running back from a road, with paths separating their two or three hectares from neighbouring holdings. As basic foods they grow green matoke bananas, sweet potatoes, cassava, maize, and various vegetables; sugar cane, pineapples, pawpaws and mangoes are also grown, with coffee and cotton the chief cash crops.

Village markets are located at intervals on the road, often at a road junction. Here the dispersed farming population can buy other foodstuffs and domestic requirements, and occasionally sell their produce. There may also be a garage, school, or dispensary. The functions of these small service centres is described in more detail on p. 28.

Among the influences on the rural settlement are, therefore, the physical restrictions of infertile uplands and swampy valleys, the advantages of well-drained middle slopes with mixed soils, and climatic conditions allowing a wide range of food and cash crops to be grown. However, the pattern of dispersed settlement, with individual small-holdings and road-villages, must be related to strong tribal unity and custom as well as to the configuration of the landscape.

In many cases a very rough zonal arrangement of land-use can be seen, with food crops in daily use near the homestead, annual cash crops, like cotton, beyond, and the rougher pasture where the land rises more steeply. However, other considerations may disturb this arrangement: vegetables and cotton are sometimes grown between young coffee bushes, and bananas may act as shade for the coffee. In broader, flatter areas, holdings may be arranged in depth, though the general alignment of settlement persists (Fig. 30).

Dispersed Homesteads and Market Villages

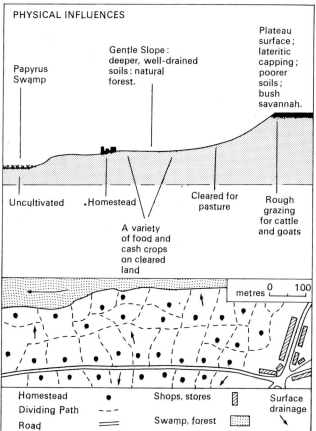

PHYSICAL INFLUENCES

Papyrus Swamp

Gentle Slope: deeper, well-drained soils: natural forest.

Plateau surface; lateritic capping; poorer soils; bush savannah.

Uncultivated

Homestead

Cleared for pasture

Rough grazing for cattle and goats

A variety of food and cash crops on cleared land

metres 0 100

Homestead •
Dividing Path - - -
Road ═══

Shops, stores ▨
Swamp, forest ▨

Surface drainage ➘

Fig. 30. (Section) *The broad relationships between slopes, soils, and forms of land-use.* (Plan) *Smallholdings near Kasangati, where a ridge drains to swampy valleys.*

Fig. 31. (above, right) *Small-holding, with bananas and maize near the home, cassava beyond, and coffee with some vegetables beyond this.*

Fig. 32. (below) *A typical market township east of Kampala, with small shops, storehouses and garage along, in this case, the main road, serving a dispersed rural population.*

Rural Communications and Transport

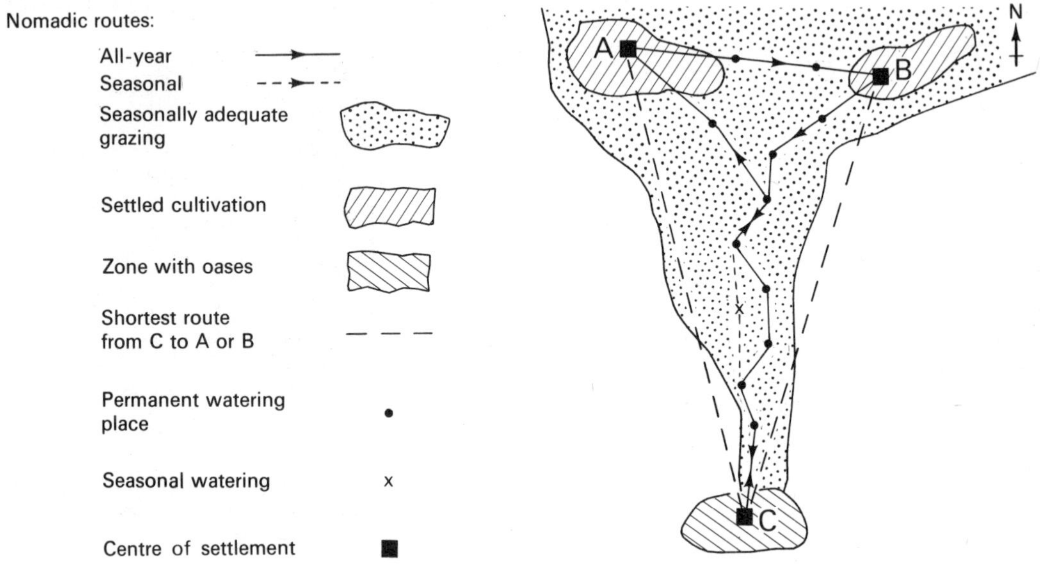

Nomadic routes:

All-year →

Seasonal - - →- - -

Seasonally adequate grazing

Settled cultivation

Zone with oases

Shortest route from C to A or B - - -

Permanent watering place •

Seasonal watering ×

Centre of settlement ■

Fig. 33. Trade routes of many hundreds of kilometres between near-coastal towns A and B and oasis settlement C respond to needs for water, grazing, and for visits to three markets. Physical obstacles or political boundaries might cause further deviations.

Development of Communications

In any group of settlements men create inter-communications—paths between houses and hamlets. From houses men travel daily to places of work, and for farmers the time required for journeys to and from the land is an important consideration. Journey-time depends on the mode of transport, the distance, and the terrain, and is a vital factor in geographical studies of settlement. Chapter V considers its effects on developing settlement patterns.

Some routes become well established; though, with land communications especially, they do not often follow a straight path between two connected places. We may therefore consider what factors cause men to adopt particular paths.

Nomadic Groups and Routes

Whereas simple hunting/gathering communities carry their own weapons and personal possessions, this is not usually so with nomadic and semi-nomadic peoples, who use forms of animal transport. There are thus more complex factors affecting the paths followed by the latter, especially if they come to carry goods for other peoples.

As we have seen, wandering herdsmen seasonally follow broad routes between series of watering places and travel corridors of suitable grazing land. They transport various goods—food, fodder and materials for shelter, according to needs and customs. Many nomads add the role of carriers of goods for peoples along the route to that of herdsmen. Some have come to act as merchants and middlemen. In the Libyan desert, and elsewhere in North Africa, they transport cereals, vegetables, vegetable oils, and cattle to oases, and there exchange them for dates, which they sell at near-coastal settlements.

Fig. 33 shows, diagrammatically, how various influences may act to establish a nomadic route between such near-coastal settlements and an oasis. The forces acting are the extent of the corridor of adequate grazing; the locations of the cultivated areas

A, B, and the oasis C; the goods and services A and B can provide for C, and vice versa; and the location of reliable watering places. The route is seen to deviate from straight-line connections.

The actual route taken will depend on the transport used and the conditions along the way. A camel train, needing to visit fewer watering points, would be likely to take a more direct route than pack donkeys with cattle. Seasonal changes of vegetation and the drying of certain water-holes might lengthen the route. A modern road built direct between AC or BC would probably affect the whole way of life of the nomadic carriers.

Fixed Settlements—Route Deviations

Tracks soon develop about a settlement, to and from fields, wells, or sources of wood or stone, and between neighbouring settlements. Again, routeways between pairs of settlements often deviate from the path of shortest distance.

Routeways and Journey-Time

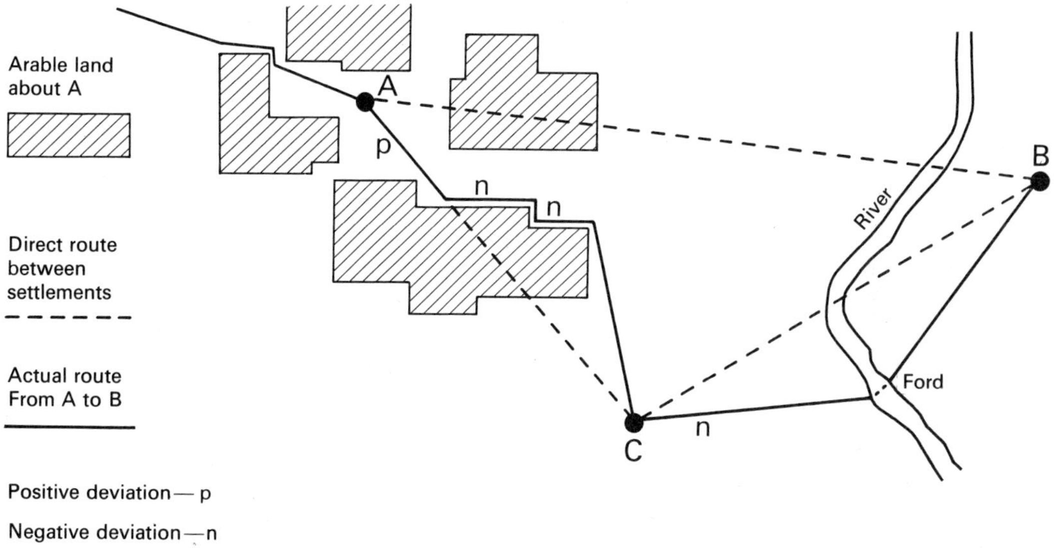

Arable land
about A

Direct route
between
settlements

- - - - - -

Actual route
From A to B

_____

Positive deviation— p

Negative deviation—n

Fig. 34. Traffic from, and passing through A has a positive advantage in visiting C on the way to B ; the deviation at A is a positive one (p). Negative deviations (n) are made to avoid fields and deep-water crossing. A devious route is thus imprinted on the landscape.

Deviations from the straight line may be described as *positive* where the route is deliberately lengthened to provide an advantage (Fig. 34—A to C on the way to B), and as *negative* where deviation is advisable to avoid obstacles (existing fields between A and B; deep water between B and C).

Surfaced Tracks and Roads

The nature of the surface depends on the form of transport, the economic demands of settlement, the amount of traffic, and physical elements—climatic, geological and topographical.

Even primitive wheeled transport requires a resistant surface. But construction and maintenance are expensive in materials, time, and labour. In some areas, like the alluvial plains of northern India and the Argentine pampas, road metal (stone) is not readily available. Ruts develop, making travel slow, and perhaps impossible after rain. Yet this form of routeway is typical of much of the earth's surface.

Remember that in Britain, and much of Western Europe, main routes, let alone rural tracks, were often in a dreadful state up to the early nineteenth century. Even today, the bullock cart is a common form of transport over much of the earth's surface.

Journey-Time and Settlement Distribution

The mode of transport and state of surface affect the distance man may travel in a day, and in rural communities can influence the spacing of market centres, and hence the whole pattern of settlement (p. 101).

In medieval England (as in present-day rural India) a man on foot, or with pack animals, could manage about 12 km portage a day, allowing time spent in the market: so small markets served an area of only about 6 km radius.

Improvements of roads and vehicles extended the range of rural transport and led to trade passing through fewer markets, which were more widely spaced and offered better commercial facilities; by the nineteenth century the spacing of market towns in the English Midlands averaged some 20 km.

Dispersed settlement induces a greater length of route (and water pipes and electric cables). Thus modern, planned settlements, as on the Dutch polders, have systems of roads and utilities which aim to minimise overall distances.

Route Planning and Rural Settlement

New routeways can profoundly affect settlement in fringing areas. In Roman Britain, arterial routes, which still survive in the modern network, made for firm control, encouraged long-distance trade, and supplied outer provinces. Romano-British tributary routes aided agrarian development, much as Brazil's long trunk-road from Belem to Brasilia now encourages settlement on land once too remote for commercial agriculture. Planned routes may also by-pass settlements, but see p. 92.

25

Commercial Central Places

Fig. 35. Ingiriya has developed as a small market town where the road from Colombo to Ratnapura meets that from Panadure on the south-west coast of Ceylon. Its open-fronted shops supply the closely populated rural area, from which its storehouses (right) *receive and distribute surplus rice, coir and spices.*

Market Functions

The following pages consider those settlements which provide services for a productive rural population living in individual farms or for small, nucleated farming communities. Here we discuss two such central places, serving their immediate surroundings. Each has advantages of position; each at a road junction, connected to a major city and port; each has a strong market function, with business men depending on local farmers for their livelihood. Ingiriya is small; one of a number of townships spaced over a productive lowland. Arusha is larger, offers more services, has a wider commercial field, but is still very much of the local countryside.

About Ingiriya, between the piedmont ridge-and-valley country and the coastal flats of south-west Ceylon, the people live in hamlets and small villages beside broad valleys covered with paddy, among coconut palms and groves of rubber trees. The gardens of small-holdings have a variety of plants—palms, roots, spices, fruits. Household requirements, cloth, oil, and fish from the coast can be obtained at Ingiriya, and surplus rice, coir, spices, etc., is delivered there. At Ingiriya the market function is dominant.

Arusha, south of Mt. Meru, has coastal road and rail links with Tanga and Mombasa, and roads crossing dry savannahs to Nairobi and Dodoma. From an old trading post it has become a regional administrative centre for rich coffee-growing lands on the volcanic soils of northern Tanzania. It has several distinct commercial functions: its retail shops and storehouses reflect regional agricultural prosperity; its role as a tourist base is shown by its hotels and garages; and it also retains its function as a local market centre. The stalls of its open market serve families arriving by bus from prosperous farming districts and those who have walked in from dry grasslands to purchase cloth, implements, spices, etc., and to sell small items of produce.

Fig. 36. Part of the large open market at Arusha in northern Tanzania. Notice the bananas and vegetables, and the gourd used as a container. These are farming families and pastoralists who have travelled in from surrounding districts, most to buy, some to sell small items.

Larger Rural Settlements

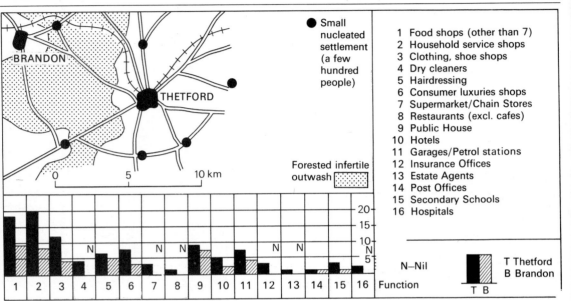

Fig. 37. Selected functions associated with different ranks of rural town (Thetford—population about 6,000; Brandon—about 4,000). The towns are separated by infertile Breckland, each serving smaller settlements in an agricultural countryside though, like some other East Anglian settlements, Brandon's functions have been influenced by a nearby air-base. The larger place has a number of functions which do not occur at all in the smaller; its greater number of functional units is probably indicative of a wider service hinterland, rather than its larger urban population.

Legend for functions:
1 Food shops (other than 7)
2 Household service shops
3 Clothing, shoe shops
4 Dry cleaners
5 Hairdressing
6 Consumer luxuries shops
7 Supermarket/Chain Stores
8 Restaurants (excl. cafes)
9 Public House
10 Hotels
11 Garages/Petrol stations
12 Insurance Offices
13 Estate Agents
14 Post Offices
15 Secondary Schools
16 Hospitals

Forested infertile outwash

N–Nil   T Thetford   B Brandon

The Growth of Market Centres

In times of general prosperity and increasing population, some rural centres, which receive the produce and supply the needs of agricultural communities, prosper and grow in competition with others. On a large area with uniform conditions such a centre would need to trade with and provide services for a certain number of farms, hamlets and villages, within a radius which would partly depend on the available form of transport; those beyond that radius would rely on some other market centre. Pages 97–101 consider the spacing of such small rural towns and the overall settlement pattern.

But, of course, there is seldom uniformity of relief or land-use, nor a regular distribution of hamlets, villages and towns. In southern Uganda (p. 22) the exact location of market towns relates to relief, water-supplies, and drainage. Market townships are often on a ridge, avoiding the better farmland, with a fresher atmosphere than the valley bottoms, and

usually at the junction of roads which front the small farms. Here are groups of shops, stores, cafés, garages, welfare clinics, and perhaps a small cotton ginnery. A study of the functions and services that such places offer usually reveals their relative importance as settlements.

Advantages of position and site—have often led to major urban development: Rouen at its estuary head, Shrewsbury in its meander loop, and Apennine route towns to the south of the Po Valley. Even the smallest towns respond to local physical influences, which should be recognised; though generally there is little value in labelling them 'gap' or 'route' towns simply for classification.

Functions and Services

A study of functions helps us to understand the role of a place in the overall settlement pattern. A small village will house local farmworkers, a few craftsmen, and maybe a general storekeeper, and has certain

functions depending on its region—in England, perhaps a church, post office, several small shops, and a pub offer services. But a market town is likely to have a wider range of functions which occur in greater number (more functional units). There are likely to be more shops—grocers, butchers, chemists, and other small retail stores—inns and cafés, garages, district school, bank, solicitor's office, and administrative buildings, depending on the size of the rural area it serves, the sophistication of the population, and its relative accessibility.

Usually a certain minimum population is needed for a settlement to support a certain function. Whether it *will* be there depends on individual circumstances: a market town on a busy highway may have several service stations and a motel, unlike its neighbouring towns. But, despite variations, functions are valuable indicators of settlement status (p. 97). Here we consider rural settlements—towns which retain their characteristic inter-relations with the surrounding countryside.

Planned Rural Settlement

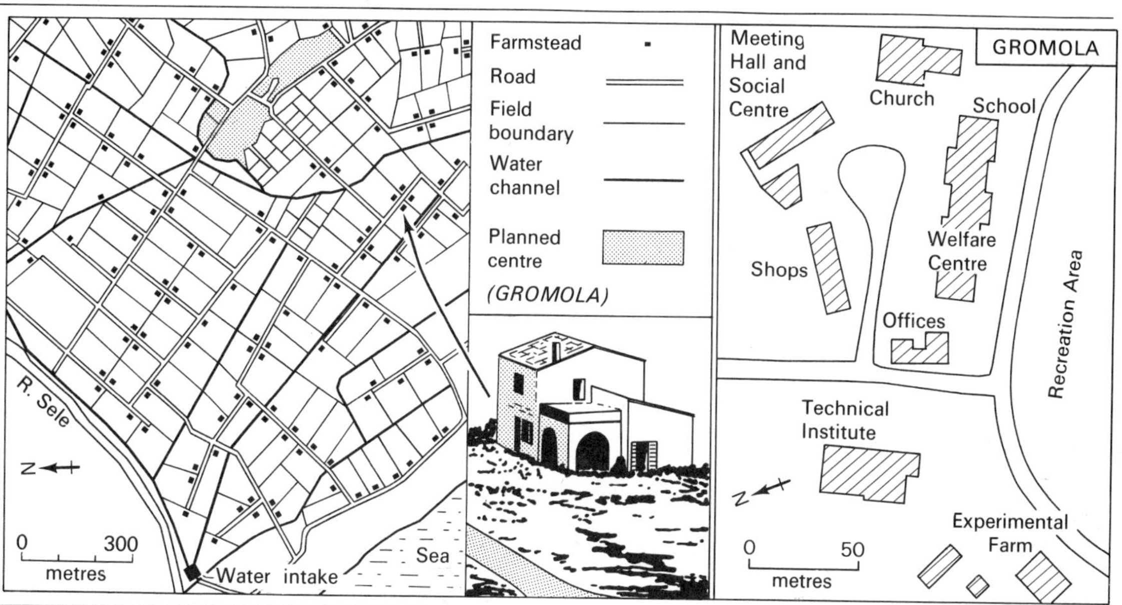

Fig. 38. Planned settlement on the Sele River plain, south of Naples, where the Board for the Development of Southern Italy has provided farmsteads on reclaimed land about the township of Gromola, created as an administrative, service and social centre. New factories process agricultural produce (tomatoes, for instance) and provide work for men and women in an area where few can find employment in secondary industries.

Regional Characteristics

A market town will generally show recognisable regional characteristics; outwardly, rural towns in, say, Uganda, Ceylon, Australia, or England have distinctive appearance and form. Common features will be those related to the market function and the services offered. Thus, the open space of the original market is usually near the town centre, and nearby a wide main street flanked by shops and stores—whether those beneath the shady arcades of a North African suq, the open shop fronts of an Indonesian bazaar, or the glass-fronted display rooms of an English 'High Street'.

Visible signs of other functions and services may add regional colour—the spires of English churches, the domes of mosques; the Australian sports oval and bowling green, the Indian maidan (square for games and leisure), or a Spanish bull-ring. Traditional styles of architecture are also found in the older administrative buildings.

Of course, with time and the increasing ease of distribution of cultural ideas and building materials, towns a hemisphere apart begin to display common features, a universal style seen in modern office blocks, garages, cinemas and motels.

Planned Rural Settlement

Not all rural settlements are the spontaneous creation of generations of countryfolk. Many who work on the land live in groups of houses planned and sited by the owners of an estate or plantation, or as part of a government-sponsored scheme. The uniformity of appearance of the streets in and about Woburn, in mid-Bedfordshire, is due to the successive provisions of cottages and houses by agents of the Dukes of Bedford. Plantation employees in India and Ceylon often live in 'lines' somewhat resembling those of an Eastern military cantonment. In contrast to this, other organisations may encourage variety (see Fig. 41).

In southern Italy the work of the Casa per il Mezzogiorno (for the development of the South) has drained coastlands, like the Metaponto Plain, eradicated malaria, provided gravity-fed and pumped water, and created individual farms, set in small plots, for farmers from the overcrowded 'agro-towns' and hill villages. Commercial, social and religious amenities are provided in small townships created amid the reclaimed land. However, it is instructive to note that, despite the obvious advantages, there was much dissatisfaction at first from older men, used to gregarious living in hill-top towns, where, despite long journeys to poor fields, they preferred the social life to the loneliness of an isolated farm and the 'coldness' of a planned centre. Social factors are important considerations in any rural planning. In Dutch reclamation schemes, dwellings are usually in village units rather than in isolation, for social reasons as well as for compactness and land conservation.

Functions and Services

Fig. 39. Ravensthorpe lies in the south-eastern part of the wheat-sheep belt of Western Australia; a small central place serving surrounding agricultural districts and those engaged locally in copper mining. There is some through traffic on the road between Albany and Esperance, which links with the roads across the Nullarbor and to Kalgoorlie.

Its functions and services are typical of such inland settlements. A hotel and stores stand near the crest of the hill, with filling station and repair shops, post office, and a surgery close by. But for high-priced goods, and for cultural or recreational purposes, local people and the farmers of the wider hinterland make occasional journeys to Albany, Esperance, or even Perth, six hundred kilometres away.

Planned Settlement

Many planned settlements are constructed in their entirety by architects and builders, for estate owners or government contractors. Colonia Campanilla, in Puerto Rico, is an interesting example of how individuality may be maintained. Necessities are provided—water supply, planned drainage, road layout, power, house foundations—and loans are available on easy terms for workers on the sugar estates; but the latter have freedom to make what they will of the superstructure and amenities of their holdings. The result is a settlement with personalities and temperaments reflected in the housing, as one might find in any village community.

Fig. 41. Part of Colonia Campanilla, a township for sugar estate employees in the coastal sugar-growing countryside of northern Puerto Rico.

Fig. 40. The position of Ravensthorpe.

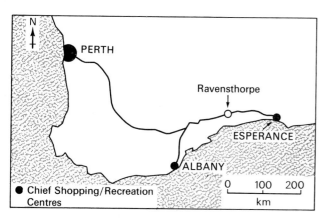

31

Chapter III
Agricultural Systems

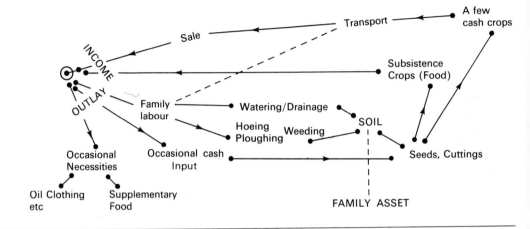

⊙ —The Family

Fig. 42. Here and in Figs. 43, 47, 48, we examine different forms of farming organisation, and the relationships between families, labourers, and managerial staff and the soil from which the produce is derived.

Lines join many of the inter-related factors which act on one another, and help to emphasise that so much more than simple crop-soil-climatic relationships are involved in making a living, or a profit, from the land.

Settlement and Forms of Agriculture

Settlement, as opposed to nomadism, involves cultivation and systems of agricultural land-use. These vary, from the practices of simple societies to those used to supply distant commercial markets. The spatial patterns of settlement are closely bound up with various systems of agriculture; so at this point we may consider how men cultivate the land.

Peasants and Farmers

Millions of cultivators are self-employed and use only family labour. They have little capital to invest in the small area they farm. They consume much of their produce, but may have a small surplus for sale or barter. These are *peasant* cultivators, and differ from 'small farmers' only in the amount of their land and that they do not employ labour, nor, generally, expect much of a surplus. There is, however, no clear-cut definition of a 'peasant cultivator'. Many

are tenants, but land-ownership is not a distinguishing factor.

Farmers, as distinct from peasants, are also frequently tenants. Often the landlord provides various items of 'fixed capital', including the buildings, while the tenant provides livestock, seed-grain, fertiliser, machinery and so on. This enables the forward-looking farmer to invest capital in improving the quality of these possessions.

In communist countries the farmer-worker serves the community as a whole, and there is little private ownership, though workers on Russian collectives may farm private plots as well.

SYSTEMS OF FARMING

The numbers employed on the land and the time devoted to farming vary with peoples' state of development, technological aids and available capital, their choice of crops or animals, and, of course, with soil fertility, climatic factors, and the terrain itself.

Subsistence Farming with Settled Tillage

Large areas of central Africa, South and Central America, and south-east Asia are farmed by families, whose small plots, receiving little fertiliser, need fallow periods, and yield mainly for family consumption, perhaps producing a little for sale. Individual families strive to grow a variety of foods according to the region—bananas, yams, cassava, maize, beans, and pumpkins in the moist tropics; in drier locations, millet, beans, and oilseeds; they may also own a few domestic fowl and pigs.

Houses and separate, small foodstores are usually of local materials. Agricultural tools are simple—the most common is the broad iron blade, fixed to a wooden handle.

Many sell surplus food, spices or oilseeds; but it is difficult to distinguish purely subsistence family farming from profit-seeking small-holders. Much depends on the time devoted to producing cash

PLANTATION
FARMING

⊙ —The Owners

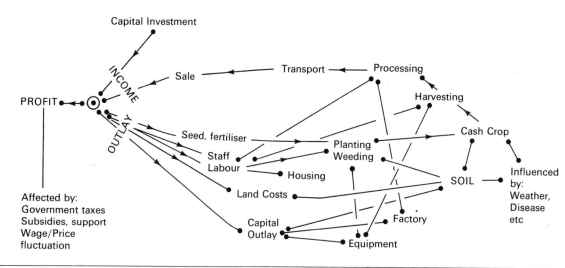

Fig. 43. A simplification of the items of outlay and income involved in a plantation system of farming, employing managerial staff and indigenous or foreign labour. This does not take into account the complex political and social problems which are apt to arise in this type of organisation.

crops: where this exceeds, say, 25 per cent., it is doubtful if the life is simple 'subsistence farming'.

Intensive Subsistence Farming

Where the pressure of peasant population is great, much time and effort must be devoted to obtaining the maximum possible yield of food crops with available techniques and tools. Abundant labour is the chief input.

In Monsoon Asia, for instance, deltas, plains and terraced hills, flooded during the rains, yield one or two rice crops, and sometimes also a dry season crop of wheat, barley, pulses or vegetables. The contiguous patterns of small fields, and lines of contoured terraces, reflect the need to use all available land. Less suitable land may bear tree crops and carry most of the settlements—often on slopes too steep to cultivate, or on embankments beside waterways, taking up as little cultivable land as possible.

Commercial Plantation Agriculture

Most plantations were established to provide tropical and sub-tropical commodities to temperate industrial countries. Much labour is needed to prepare, grow, harvest and process produce for export. Europeans and Americans engaged cheap manual labour, able to work in local conditions—though not necessarily local people.

Most plantation crops are also grown by independent farmers. For large-scale production, however, much capital is required—for clearing, drainage, irrigation, providing roads, vehicles, water supply, power, housing, schools, hospitals, for riding the period after initial planting and before production, and for land management.

There are dangers within the system. A single crop cultivated continuously exhausts soils; and is vulnerable as a whole to disease. Social stresses are invited by the nature of plantation organisation, and

political factors are often involved.

The overall pattern of settlement is huge areas of monoculture, amid which are large central buildings, processing plant, housing of managerial staff, and clustered 'lines' of labourers and families, who may have plots for cultivation. In some cases labour comes from nearby 'satellite' villages.

Extensive Commercial Farming

Where land is fertile, plentiful, and relatively cheap, but labour scarce, a large output is achieved by cultivating a wide area through mechanisation.

Grain Farming. Extensive grain farming in North America and Australia, for example, uses much machinery and transport systems capable of handling bulk produce, from storage elevators amid farmlands to bulk terminals at docksides. Family labour, or travelling teams operate harvesters and mechanical aids; so few permanent settlers are needed.

Extensive Pastoral Farming

Fig. 44. The homestead of Paroo station in Western Australia, amid red-earth plains, close to the limits of agricultural settlement; its land borders the No. 1 Rabbit Fence, some eighty kilometres from the small service township, part 'ghost mining-town' of Wiluna. Here the family farms some two hundred thousand hectares of leased land—one sheep per forty hectares; sheep survive the droughts on mulga seeds and grass growth after occasional storms. Experience, manual dexterity, and endurance enable the farmer and his sons to make a living, with the help of aboriginal shearers, and occasional visits of the 'dogger' to put down the dingoes.

Monoculture is usual on plantations, and here most of the hillsides are covered in close rows of tea bushes; but a large work force is used for the continuous rotation picking and processing, so that intensive food cultivation is often found side by side with the cash crop.

In the central highlands of Ceylon the middle slopes are usually used for tea cultivation and drain down to the lower slopes and valley floors, where most of the food crops are grown.

Many workers live in accommodation provided close to the factory, but some in clusters of houses with their own plots, and others in small villages with a community centre, temple, and other amenities. Similar variations can be seen about the tea estates in the Kenya Highlands.

Fig. 45. (above) The moist green landscape of a tea plantation near Nuwara Eliya in the central highlands of Ceylon. Roads through tea-covered hillsides converge on the central factory and its outbuildings, where the tea is processed and packed.

Fig. 46 (below) In this part of the Ceylonese Highlands the steeper slopes and spurs are covered with dark green tea bushes and shade trees. The more gentle slopes have been carefully terraced for intensive rice growing, and in the foreground plots of vegetables and cassava are being cultivated.

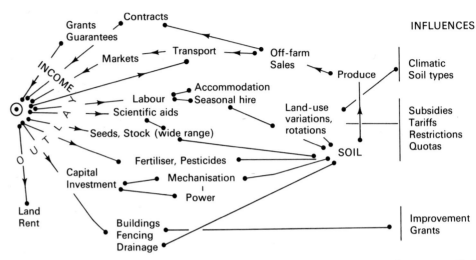

TEMPERATE
MIXED FARMING

⊙ — Family farm
(owner, tenant)

INFLUENCES

Contracts
Grants
Guarantees
Markets ← Transport → Off-farm Sales
INCOME
Accommodation
Labour → Seasonal hire
Scientific aids
Seeds, Stock (wide range)
Fertiliser, Pesticides
Capital Investment → Mechanisation
Power
Land Rent
Buildings Fencing Drainage
Produce
Land-use variations, rotations
SOIL

Climatic Soil types

Subsidies
Tariffs
Restrictions
Quotas

Improvement Grants

Fig. 47. Temperate Mixed Farming. In regions with this type of farming there is usually a wide range of produce, each subject to subsidies, grants or restrictions; local land-use and the overall distribution of crops depend on much more than simple plant-soil-climatic relationships.

In extensive grain farming the average yields per hectare are low compared with those of more intensive farming in, say, East Anglia; but the volume produced overall is very great.

In the temperate interiors of the continents extensive farming developed about the lines of the railroads, expanding laterally as communication networks were established. Farms lie within, or at the edge of, land allotments or appropriations, creating a dispersed farming population, served by fairly regularly spaced nucleated market settlements.

Extensive Stock Farming. The drier, interior parts of temperate grasslands generally support low density grazing by cattle or sheep, based on dispersed ranches or stations. The tendency in better watered prairies, steppes, or 'outback' has been towards larger numbers of animals in huge, fenced paddocks containing watering points, about a homestead amid planted shelter trees. This calls for careful selection, breeding, and treatment of stock.

In sheep farming, seasonal labour may be acquired for mustering, dipping or shearing, and grading and packing the wool; there are few permanent hands, and, again, a low population density.

In recent years more and more rotation farming is practised in these huge areas of grain and pastoral farming. In the better watered parts livestock may be combined with grain, fodder and other crops. In many cases government quotas for production contribute to changes in the form of land-use.

Commercial Livestock and Crop Production

(Temperate Mixed Farming)

The normal unit is the family farm, and most produce is sold off the farm. The farmer has several sources of income—from cash crops, feed stuffs, and livestock; this protects against variations in price

due to fluctuations in production and demand. Prevailing quotas, tariffs, and subsidies are likely to influence the choice of crops and livestock.

The form of settlement is one of small farms, using little but family labour; there is high investment in farm machinery, equipment, specialised buildings, and much outlay on fertiliser, sprays, etc. Outside Europe, this intensive form of land-use is practised in north-east America and the Mid-West Corn Belt, and in some of the more temperate parts of Australia and New Zealand.

Commercial Dairy Farming

A dairy herd must feed continuously from permanent or temporary (rotation) pastures, or from stored fodder. Pastures are usually sown with grasses, herbs, and leguminous plants according to soils and climatic conditions. The fodder comes from hay, oats, barley, or roots, stored for feed when pasture growth is at a minimum.

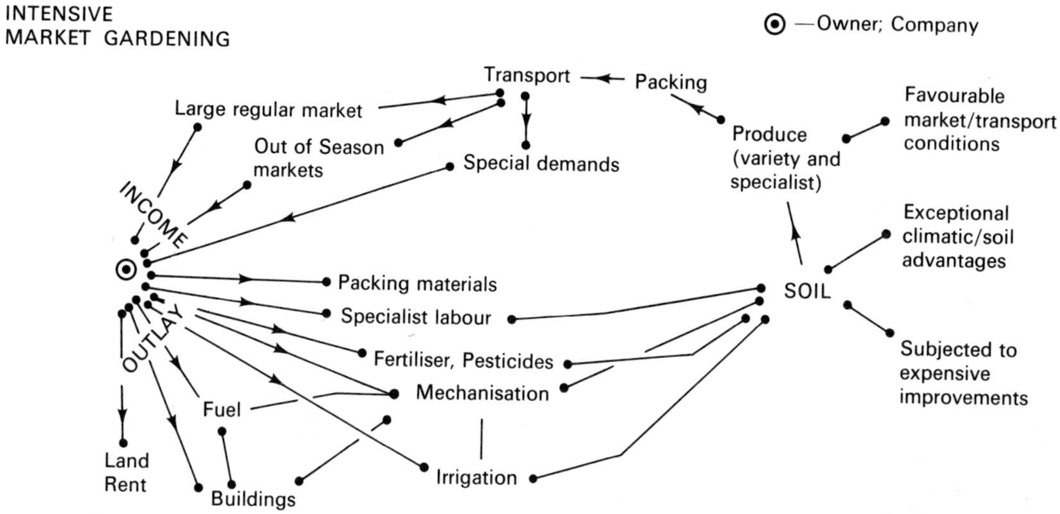

Intensive Methods

INTENSIVE
MARKET GARDENING

Fig. 48. Intensive Market Gardening. This may take place in particularly favoured climatic/soil regions, especially where there are 'out-of-season' advantages, or under highly artificial conditions where a sufficiently profitable market exists to warrant the large outlay.

This means storage facilities, silos, barns, and stalls on the farm: though in warm temperate lands, like New Zealand's North Island, with all-year round pasture, there is less need for fodder. In Denmark, by contrast, cattle are stall-fed in winter.

Dairy farms tend to be smaller than mixed or arable farms, and to be set in a countryside of low density, dispersed settlement. The small farmer employs few men (and is often tied to the farm), but he needs a lot of capital for buildings and machinery. Co-operative systems, with central creameries and cheese factories, suit dairying. Seed, fertiliser, and machinery are supplied to farmers, who receive profits in proportion to their contribution and shares in the co-operative.

Bulk transport can carry milk to urban centres from dairy regions a hundred kilometres away in a few hours. But more isolated regions convert much of their milk into non-perishable, easily transportable forms—mainly butter and cheese.

Intensive Market Gardening and Horticulture

Certain small areas are intensively cultivated to supply large urban markets with fruit, flowers, vegetables, and salad crops. Some areas near the market overcome disadvantages of soil and climatic conditions by using expensive glasshouses, soil heating, fertilisers and irrigation. These are used in the Sandy-Biggleswade area of Bedfordshire which has easy access to London by the A1 Motorway.

Other areas are climatically suited to particular crops or to early production. Stone fruits of the Vale of Evesham benefit from a combination of well-drained alluvial soils and a local climate with only moderately cold spells. The mild Scilly Isles send early spring flowers to London.

This type of agriculture makes for close settlement by small, but prosperous farms, often sited along or near roads, and close to the gardens and glasshouses which need so much attention.

'Mediterranean' Agriculture

Winter crops can be grown in the mild rainier season, and in the hot, dry summers other crops may be cultivated where irrigation is available. Sheep and goats may graze out all the year, transhumance often allowing alternate use of highland and lowland.

In places of ancient settlement about the Mediterranean, land-use patterns have usually evolved about villages. Crops requiring a high input of labour are grown near the village (i.e., vegetables and certain fruits); grain crops and olives beyond; and open rough grazing at a distance, pp. 72–76. These are age-old arrangements which minimise the time spent on each activity.

Lands of later settlement, with plentiful irrigation water, like California, tend to use highly mechanised cultivation, packing, and distribution, thus creating a very different landscape, with large 'factory farms' amid rectangular fields, channels, and roads.

Intensive Market Gardening

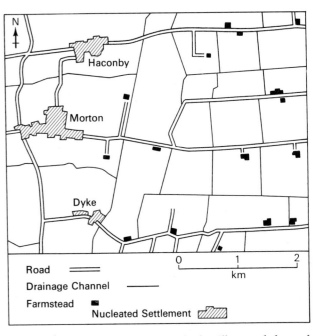

Fig. 51. *In this Lincolnshire countryside the villages and the north-south road stand some ten metres above the level fen to the east. Notice the network of channels and roads, somewhat above field level, and the farmhouses dispersed over this intensively cultivated land.*

Fig. 49. (above) *Intensive farming calls for careful management. Beside the glasshouse on this level Norfolk fen farm, near Outwell, boxes are neatly stacked, ready for fruit picking to begin.*

Fig. 50 (below) *Intensive farming near Wisbech, where flowers are grown both for cutting and seed; beyond the fruit trees are fields of soft fruits, picked in mid-summer.*

The main characteristics of intensive commercial farming are stressed on pages 36 and 37. There is usually heavy investment in the land and a high product yield per unit area. This type of farming is generally associated with high living standards and large urban markets.

When land is used intensively, care must be taken to ensure that the soil fertility and soil structure do not deteriorate. Deterioration is apt to occur slowly and insidiously and then become serious under certain conditions. The fertility of many fen soils, such as those in Fig. 52, have been based on a high organic content, built up under peat-forming conditions and made available to crops through draining, ploughing and aerating the soil. In time, the texture of many fen soils has become so fine that, under dry conditions, wind, which blows unchecked across the fenland, and is itself a drying agent, can remove the top-soil.

Fig. 52. Settlement on the fens east of Ely, showing part of the drainage system. The isolated farmhouse and buildings stand in a clump of trees amid the closely cultivated fields, which are sown and harrowed mechanically. Some fen crops, however, notably fruits, need a large seasonal labour force. At picking time some farmers house migrant pickers in caravans, or provide hutted accommodation.

Chapter IV
Urban Development

The Beginnings

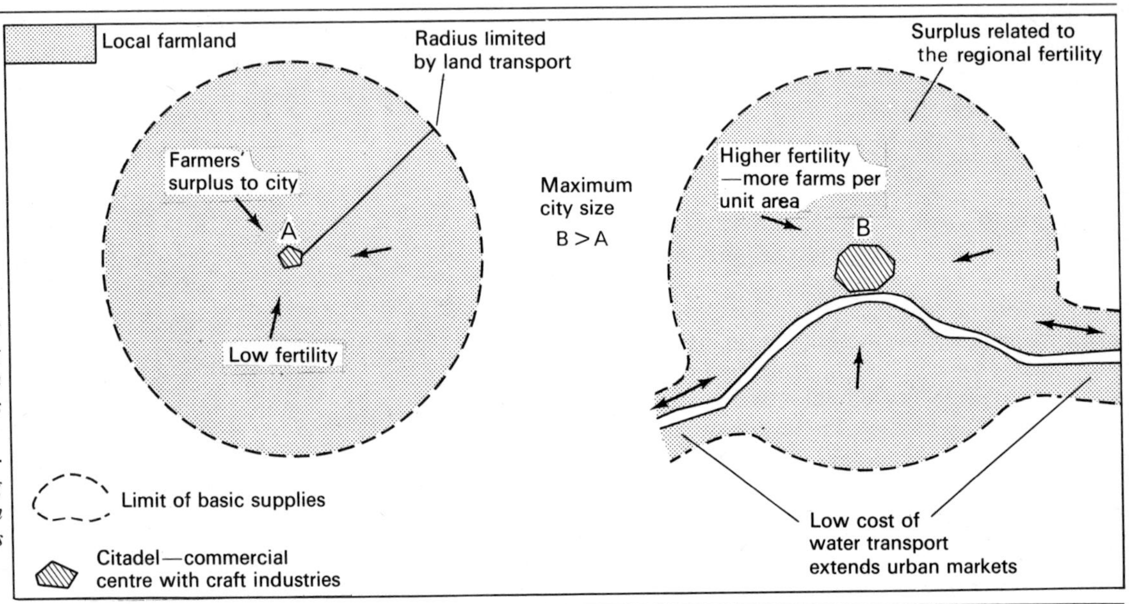

Fig. 53. The population of an ancient city, living within its walls, drew on the surplus produce of farming families living within an economic radius; a distance which depended on the forms of transport available and the type of commodities provided.

Many ancient cities benefited from the use of water transport. Here B, being in a more fertile region (and assuming equal ability among farmers) receives a larger surplus than A, and has the advantage of river transport to widen its commercial field.

Labels in figure:
- Local farmland
- Radius limited by land transport
- Surplus related to the regional fertility
- Farmers' surplus to city
- Higher fertility —more farms per unit area
- Maximum city size B > A
- Low fertility
- Limit of basic supplies
- Citadel—commercial centre with craft industries
- Low cost of water transport extends urban markets

Early Settlement and Functions

We have seen that as commercial central places increase in size and rank they have more functions and provide more services than lower-order settlements. As settlement developed in ancient times, the urban central places were limited in size by the degree of fertility and prosperity of the surrounding region—unless they were on a major routeway.

Such towns would organise the collection and distribution of produce, trade with other regions, provide the services of potters, metal workers, and other craftsmen, and act as centres of secular and religious administration. The inhabitants thus created an 'urban' environment, with social contacts and cultural exchanges, far removed from life on the land or in the small towns and villages.

Such developments took place five or six thousand years ago on the great river plains of the Tigris and Euphrates, where cities like Babylon and Nineveh developed, and also in the Nile and Indus Valleys.

Early Trading and Manufacturing Towns

Gradually, trading centres developed beyond the areas of agricultural settlement. These acquired various necessities and luxuries from far afield—metals, salt, fibres, precious stones, amber, etc., and produced an increasing number of semi-manufactured goods made by their own craftsmen. Many were ports, such as the Phoenician Tyre and Sidon, with large trading communities. Some inland trading centres were, in a sense, 'ports of the desert', like Aleppo (Halab) and Damascus.

A third phase of development occurred when rural populations outgrew their food supplies and began either to rely on imported foods, or to migrate and found colonies elsewhere. Often, as in Greek colonisation, new rural areas were developed about a sited urban nucleus, usually a port. Together the rural and urban populations formed a 'city state', trading in olives, oil, wine and almonds.

Administrative Functions and Regional Control

All urban centres came in time to be run by administrative groups, and/or military organisations. By territorial expansion and conquest, certain cities controlled distant areas, as centres of wider administration, with greater wealth and prestige.

The Roman Empire was carefully organised to contribute to the power and wealth of the great city. Trade towns and ports already existed within the Empire; and others were created to control and administer distant territories. Towns like Lyons, at the node of an arterial road system, were of strategic value. Others, like Cologne, grew as trading towns protected by a Roman garrison.

After the Roman Empire, urban life survived in Byzantine south-eastern Europe and the Middle East, and under Moslem control, as their great Empire spread to include such large administrative and trading cities as Granada.

Before the Industrial Revolution

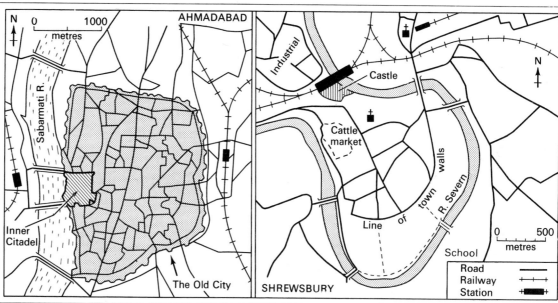

Fig. 54. In most parts of the world towns were, until quite recently, closely related to their immediate rural surroundings and walled to provide a retreat and give security for the central functions they performed.

In India, the old walled city of Ahmadabad is now capital of Gujerat, with a million inhabitants. For centuries its effective limits were walls, enclosing houses, stores and craftsmens' shops in a maze of streets. Its citadel overlooked the protective river Sabarmati. The railways, industrial zone, University, and modern suburbs now extend outwards from both sides of the river.

Compare the site of medieval Shrewsbury, protected by castle, walls, shown by the present road pattern, and the river loop. Notice the outer industrial area, railways and school, near open residential suburbs south of the river.

Urban Revival in Europe

In medieval times, stimulated by population growth and trade revival, urban life reappeared in northern Europe; but towns and cities were set in an insecure countryside, where smaller settlements were apt to be pillaged and plundered by the followers or mercenaries of a despot. Urban centres were usually fortified, and defensively sited where possible, so that tradesmen and craftsmen operated under the protection of their lord or ecclesiastical leader, who often lived in a castle within the walled town. About the towns, agricultural colonisation of forest and wasteland continued, producing an increasingly populated countryside under urban control.

Few towns in medieval Europe were large, or contained over 10 000 people. But the number of towns increased during the Middle Ages; and, as nation states developed from the maze of feudal units, their capitals grew into large metropolitan cities, from which routeways extended throughout

their lands. The influences of court patronage and wealth brought more and more functions to these capitals, whose populations rapidly increased. Most of the other urban centres remained small, their size and importance varying with their geographical location and their status—a Royal Charter would give special privileges, for example.

Certain commercial cities were exceptions, and, with ever-increasing industrial functions, ports such as Amsterdam, Antwerp, Venice, and Genoa, and inland commercial centres like Cologne, Florence and Milan, outstripped the average town.

Urban Developments Beyond Europe

Meanwhile in many parts of the world, such as the lower river basins of China and the plains of northern India, a settled rural population lived in poverty in small hamlets and villages; while the regional centres of trade and crafts, religious sites and markets, were

already the crowded irregular towns they are today.

In some parts princes ruled feudal societies from fortified towns. Already, strategically important cities, like Delhi and Peking, were predominant. The growth of mammoth cities came later, with the rapid increase of population which followed European expansion and the concentration of economic activities at a few great trading centres like Calcutta, Bombay and Shanghai.

In the Americas, European colonial towns varied. Some were enlarged trading posts, others ports acting as colonial bases. Those of strategic significance were heavily fortified and regionally dominant, like French Quebec and Spanish San Juan, Puerto Rico. Many Spanish colonial towns were laid out to standard plans drawn up in Spain, one reason why so many Spanish colonial towns were re-sited later. Sometimes indigenous urban sites were redeveloped; in Cuzco, mortarless, earthquake-resistant Inca buildings formed foundations for many Spanish colonial buildings.

Fortified Towns

Fig. 55. *The walled town of M'dina in central Malta, with its cathedral standing out on the left. As its name implies, M'dina was once an Islamic citadel. The Norman conquest saw the building of its Christian Cathedral, and it long remained an ecclesiastical and administrative capital, its ramparts overlooking a countryside of small villages—a fortified retreat in times of trouble.*

It is well sited on the edge of a plateau of Corallian limestone, which forms the high surface of much of western Malta, and overlooks a broad, gently rolling surface of Globerigena limestone to the east.

Site and Security

Fig. 56. In southern Andalusia, the houses of the market centre, Casares, are clustered on the slopes of a prominent outlier (a similar feature may be seen in the background).

The Moors fortified the upper part of the hill, and the remains of castle and mosque may be seen to the right. A church now overlooks the small compact town, whose hinterland includes a number of dispersed fortified farmhouses, amid hills covered with cork oak and valleys partly cleared for olives, vines and wheat.

43

Settlement and Local Security

Strong points do not necessarily ensure the survival of local communities. They themselves may be sacked, or economic circumstances, such as enclosure, or disease, such as the Plague, may cause settlements to decline. The remains of the once-powerful castle and adjoining settlement (Fig. 57) are set in part of the English Midlands where numerous villages were abandoned following early enclosures (see also p. 98).

In particularly insecure regions towns may be created as defence centres. There are many examples in northern Italy, where rival city states built small defence-towns near their borders. Palmanova (Fig. 59) was created in a highly insecure frontier region.

Fig. 57. A motte and bailey near Lilbourne, Northamptonshire, the stronghold of the de Camvil family. Notice the markings of the medieval settlement and of the three-field system beyond the 13th century church. Foundations of old cottages lie in the copse, and the main well is seen in the field near the road junction.

Fig. 58. The position of Palmanova in Friuli—a frontier region with numerous fortresses.

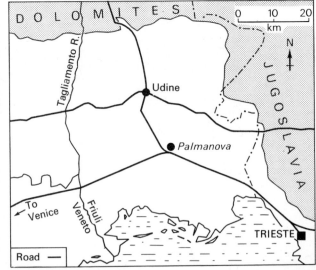

Fig. 59. Palmanova was built in 1593 about a central piazza, in a star-shaped plan designed to keep attackers as far from the town centre as possible.

In this remote region, limited resources and inheritance laws have created a rural landscape of small fragmented holdings. Palmanova remains compact and apart from the countryside; notice how the regional through-road skirts the town.

Hill Town – Overpopulation

Fig. 60. *The crowded hill-town of Matera in southern Italy, where bare limestone ridges alternate with vales of loose sandstones, difficult to cultivate.*

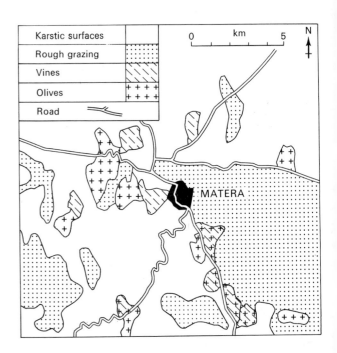

Karstic surfaces	
Rough grazing	
Vines	
Olives	
Road	

MATERA

Fig. 61. *Land-use about Matera. There is little productive arable land, and many of the olives are grown in trenches filled with artificially created soil. Rough pasture on garrigue is overgrazed by goats.*

Until the early nineteen-fifties, tens of thousands of Matera's population lived in dwellings created from caves in the limestone. The fortified hill has been the nucleus, and ruined fortifications and watch-towers can be seen embedded in the maze of houses and narrow streets, developed through the ages.

Yet people found security here in the Middle Ages, when coastal lowlands, once drained and farmed by Greeks and Romans, had become insecure, neglected, and malarial. Matera shows the advantage of a defensive site with a perched water-table, even though farmers had to travel out to cultivate difficult land, and unemployment has been, and remains, a problem.

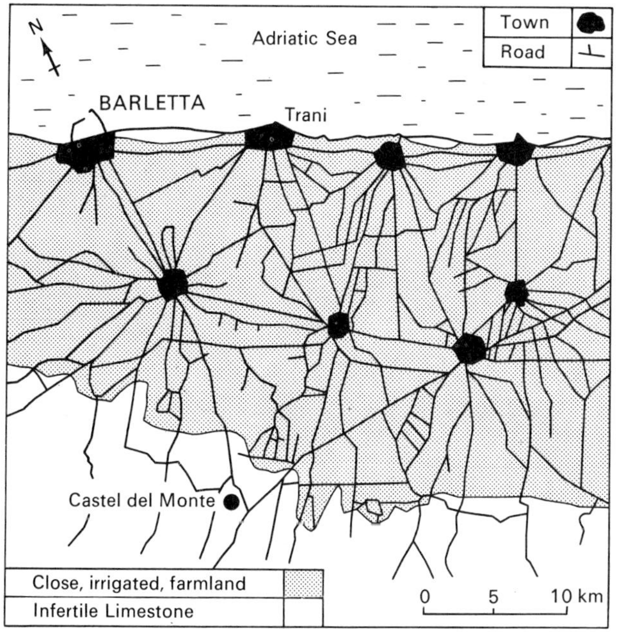

Fig. 62. *The Adriatic coast near Barletta.*

The Norman castle overlooks coastland which is now once more drained, irrigated and closely settled. Fig. 62 shows the close pattern of settlement where fertile red soils on limy sandstones support olives, vines, fruit crops, and vegetables. These coastlands were prey to marauders in the unsettled post-Roman times, and neglected channels and poor drainage allowed malaria to become a scourge. People lived rather in inland hill-towns, though, except for a few basins, the higher surfaces had little really fertile land.

Fig. 63. The view eastward from the Norman Castel del Monte, built to overlook the coastal lowlands. Beyond the poor limestones, where afforestation has failed, is the closely cultivated belt behind Trani on the Adriatic coast.

Map labels: Adriatic Sea, Town, Road, BARLETTA, Trani, Castel del Monte, Close, irrigated, farmland, Infertile Limestone, 0 5 10 km

47

Industrial Commercial Developments and Urban Growth

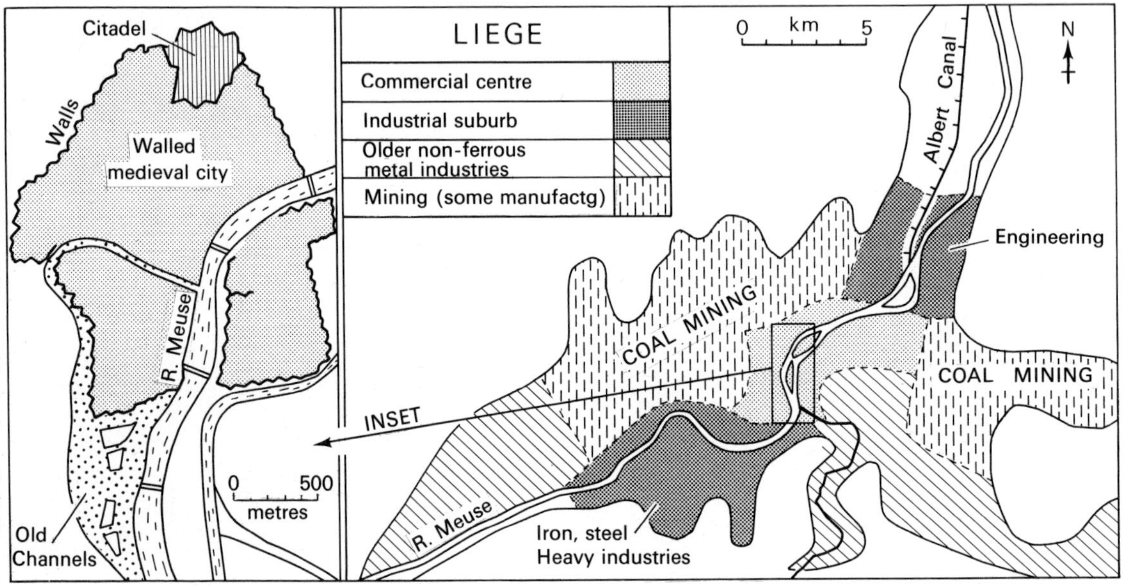

Fig. 64. The old walled city of Liege about the Meuse, a hundred metres below the plateau level, was mainly an ecclesiastical centre, with commercial and trading activities. The countryside about it was noted for coal-mining and metal working, and skilled smiths made Liege famous for nails, locks, tools, and arms.

Following the Industrial Revolution, steel production and light and heavy engineering developed in new suburbs, extending the city upstream and downstream of what has remained predominantly a commercial city centre.

We should note, however, that, as in other European countries, recent industrial development in Belgium has been at the capital city and chief port (Brussels and Antwerp) rather than at older inland centres, like Liege.

The New Industrial Towns

The divisions between rural and urban settlement have never been clear-cut. Applied scientific techniques of the Industrial Revolution complicated the distinctions and saw the growth of towns with dominant industrial functions.

In Britain, agricultural mechanisation, crop rotations, and a new wave of land-enclosures increased food output, but the agricultural labour force diminished. Food was being shipped to Europe from lands recently colonised. Agricultural workers thus released moved into towns and cities where new manufacturing enterprises, powered by steam and, later, electricity, needed industrial labour.

Workers' houses clustered near factories in terraced rows. The large industrial towns, served by a network of roads, railways and canals, were the new environment for millions, now entirely divorced from the land.

Urban Developments Following Colonisation

In the Americas. Much of the early urban growth was about the city-ports and in near-coastal settlements, for example Boston and the small industrial towns of New England, Philadelphia, New Orleans, and, in South America, Salvador, Rio de Janeiro, and Lima—though large Spanish-Indian cities existed in high Andean basins.

In North America westwards movements brought settlement along the waterways. St. Louis, on the Mississippi and Cincinatti, on the Ohio, were established by the mid-eighteenth century. The canal link through the Mohawk Gap from the Hudson river to Lake Erie, completed in 1825, opened up what was to become a major region of urban industrial development about the Great Lakes.

By 1830 more than a quarter of the USA population was west of the Appalachians, and the railways accelerated the westward flow of people as they spread over the central plains, with their developing grid patterns of roads. An urban hierarchy gradually developed, usually comprising groups of small local towns, bigger regional centres, and large cities with specific locational advantages, like Kansas City and Indianapolis. Some route-centres of western settlement became regional cities—Salt Lake City, Santa Fe; while the first rapid growth of the west coast terminal ports—San Francisco, Los Angeles, Seattle, Vancouver—came during the last half of the nineteenth century.

In Other Countries. Very many of the large towns in countries colonised by Europeans are ports which, as trade outlets and commercial centres, developed early on—Mombasa, Accra, Djakarta. In Africa south of the Sahara, large urban growth in the interior is essentially of the twentieth century—Nairobi, Salisbury, Johannesburg—though initial settlement was somewhat earlier, and some trading cities, like Kano in Nigeria, are of ancient origin.

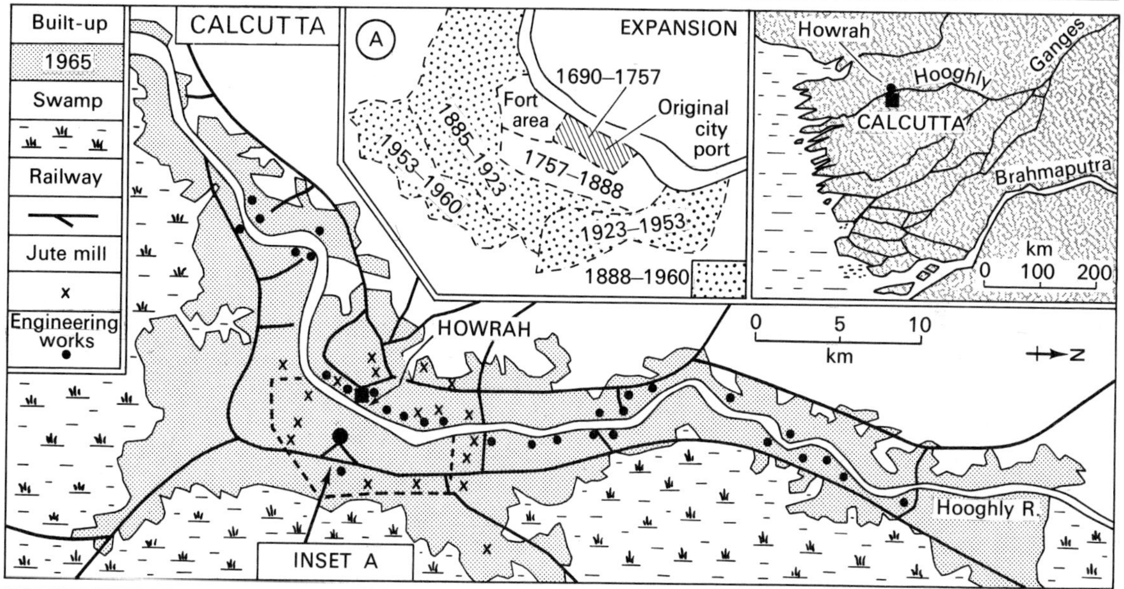

World-Wide Urban Developments

Fig. 65. Calcutta: a colonial port-city, grown to a grossly over-populated urban sprawl.

Founded on a levée of the Hooghly river on the edge of a deltaic swamp, it was the first Asian city to be developed as a nodal service centre for exports. Its location was commercially advantageous, but its site is sodden and unstable and does not improve as the city spreads eastward. It has remained commercial rather than industrial, though numerous jute mills are fed by a network of waterways and small engineering works have spread along the line of the river. Its population has immense natural growth, and as more people pour in, large numbers of its six or seven million inhabitants are without employment and lack proper water supply, sanitation, and shelter.

In Australia, the five mainland city-ports have acted as outlets for primary produce from a productive hinterland of low density settlement. With increasing population and industralisation they have become huge, multi-functional cities, with commercial, social and recreational attractions. Today, more than half the country's population lives in these five cities. Sydney and Melbourne, in particular, have widespread expanding suburbs about a high-rise business centre. Excluding these, however, there are less than twenty places in the country with a population over 25 000, and almost half these are ports.

Urban Growth in Eastern Asia

The pattern described above persists in the East. The chief ports trading with Europe are great cities—Bombay, Calcutta, Colombo, Bangkok, Saigon, Singapore and others. They contain many of the worst features of overcrowding within their large human agglomerations, into which families still migrate from poor, over-populated agricultural communities in their hinterlands.

Within these countries, as we have seen, large towns have developed in closely settled rural districts, with market and small craft industrial functions to the fore. Some are particular religious centres, like Banaras; many are regional administrative cities, like Lahore, Poona, Kuala Lumpur, or Chungking, and have outgrown other inland towns.

Japan, its settlement feudally structured until the mid-nineteenth century, now has some of the world's densest urban areas. Industrial city-port functions are spread among the conurbations of the narrow coastlands, whose development, with that of satellite towns, is further discussed in Chapter VII.

Russia—Contrasts in Urban Growth

The USSR exhibits most features of urban growth already discussed. Western Russia, until early in this century, was chiefly rural, with some market and commercial towns developing into regional capitals, with spreading suburbs; but they were still essentially of the country. Many ancient towns, like Moscow and Kiev, were on rivers, especially along the Volga. Leningrad had its origin as a western outlet port. With the advent of the railways, industrial towns developed in the Ukraine and Urals. Overall, therefore, Western Russia has the same pattern of rural-urban towns and mining-industrial centres as the rest of western Europe.

In Soviet Asia, pioneer settlement followed the Trans-Siberian railway. Mineral exploitation has created industrial settlements, and at times forced settlement has helped to populate large towns. On the once-remote shores of Lake Baikal, there are now mining and industrial towns. At Ulan Bator in Inner Mongolia an almost wholly Asiatic population lives in a technological urban environment, contrasting strongly with open expanses still populated by nomadic groups. Elsewhere, new towns have grown alongside ancient ones, as at Tashkent.

Urban Growth – Independence of Rural Surroundings

Fig. 66. New extensions of the steelworks at Ebbw Vale stretch along the valley, beside the lines of older houses, in this northern part of the South Wales coalfield. Power-lines run through sheep-farming countryside on the hills above the town.

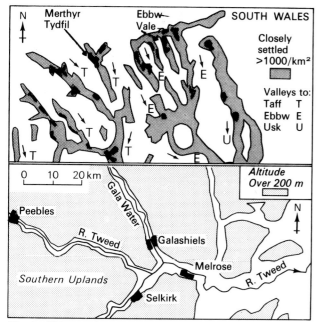

Fig. 67. Urban settlement in a rural setting.

As mining and iron and steel works were established in the valleys of South Wales, long lines of small terraced houses were built as close to the mines and factories as possible, and near railways which ran down the valleys, converging ultimately on the ports. In many cases tips from the mines have accumulated on the hillsides above the towns. Above these, however, and between each valley's line of towns, is open country.

In the Southern Uplands of Scotland water-power first located the woollen mills and associated housing within the valleys of the Tweed and its tributaries. With coal power and expanding industry, towns spread along the valleys amid countryside of great beauty.

Fig. 68. (above) *Terraced housing beside the railway in a South Wales valley.*
Fig. 69. (below) *Mills at Galashiels, along the Gala valley in the Southern Uplands.*

Urban Functions and Locational Factors

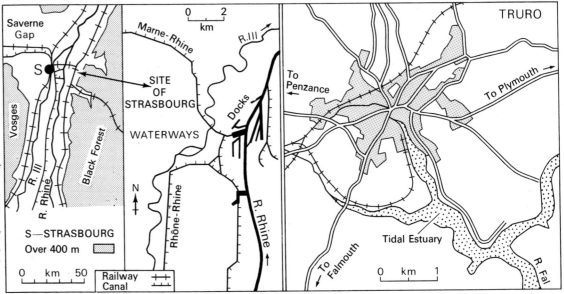

Fig. 70. At Strasbourg we see the commercial advantages of a position where communications through the Saverne Gap meet those following land- and water-routes along the Rift Valley and continuing to the industrial conurbations (p. 108) down-river.

South of Truro, the wide, tidal ria system of the Fal interrupts east-west communications, and roads and railways focus on Truro, to its great advantage as a market centre.

Towns as Multifunctional Places

Any town naturally includes a variety of functions. Markets, churches, industrial firms, bus depots, banks, etc., function to serve townsfolk and others living within the sphere of influence of the town. It is not necessarily advantageous, or wise, to label a town in terms of a function, nor easy to define the dominant function. Town censuses may indicate large numbers employed in industry, commerce or administration, and several functions may be of comparable importance and employment in them above the national average. On the whole, functional labels—'industrial town' or 'mining town'—are apt to be vague or misleading (see also p. 105).

Nevertheless, at a particular moment one function may have strong influence on the fortunes of a settlement and shape the course of future development: thus the monastic use of local gypsum-bearing wells in brew-houses at Burton-on-Trent was extended to form the basis of a major brewing industry, which became dominant when transport improvements permitted large inward movements of barley and outward distribution of beer to wider markets.

In some cases, of course, towns have been deliberately created for a particular function—mining towns like Schefferville in Labrador, or Kambalda (p. 1); ancient military bastide towns; and modern satellite industrial or residential townships.

Commercial Functions and Locational Factors

The *commercial* or *market* function is found in most central places. Its exact nature relates to such facts as the population served, the town's prosperity or otherwise, competition from places of similar size, and demands for special goods (such as fertiliser or fencing for agricultural communities). Economic competition with other places is considered on p. 97.

Particular locational factors are important. It is understandable that the commercial function will tend to be dominant in towns at route intersections, at valley confluences, at the junction of highland and lowland, and usually where physical features cause route concentration—at the lowest bridging point on a river, or the head of an estuary (Fig. 70).

But the presence, or absence, of such advantages does not alone account for growth or decline of local trade; towns do not necessarily exist as commercial places *because* of gaps or estuaries. The strength of a town's commercial function is usually related to wider settlement patterns and the need for communications and trade between different regions. Thus a market town may flourish because it is situated at a nodal point in a pattern of trade routes established between larger commercial centres.

Situation and *site* must be carefully differentiated. A place may be well situated with easy communications with other important centres, but local siting may depend on such conditions as steep or marshy ground, or physical and climatic constrictions.

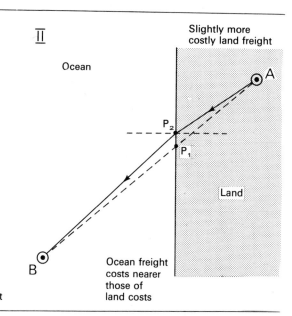

Fig. 71. Routes between A and B pass through a port P_2 sited at the least-cost location. In practice, the land- or sea-routes may deviate to collect more freight en route; and, of course, it may be physically difficult to construct a port at the theoretical location P_2.

Markets and Fairs

Towns with periodic markets and fairs have existed from early times, and in many modern British towns the weekly, or bi-weekly outdoor market still flourishes. Permanent local markets tend to supply everyday requirements to large communities; periodic markets at smaller centres may also supply special goods, and perhaps entertainments, as do periodic fairs at the larger places. Some medieval towns were noted for such fairs, often connected with religious festivals. Usually these benefited from a particular situation; some, like Leipzig, at a focal point of routes northward from the Alps and eastward from the Rhine, attracted people from great distances.

In developing countries today, periodic markets offer goods and services to people who find it difficult to travel to central place markets. Large fairs with religious festivals take place at particular locations in Asia and South America, bringing con-siderable income (and disease) to town and district, as during the mass pilgrimages to Hardwar on the upper Ganges.

In the past, prosperous commercial towns needed the security of walls and ramparts, still seen embedded in later urban growth, whether in Italian hill towns like Matera (Fig. 60) or in English lowland cities like York, or, in the old Nigerian walled city of Kano, standing adjacent to a modern commercial centre.

Commercial Ports—Locational Factors

The main functions of most sea-ports are special extensions of commercial activities. They are places of exchange between a hinterland, whose routes converge on wharves and docks, and widely distributed traders overseas. The overseas routes are proscribed and limited by economic considerations, related to the nature, bulk, and amount of commodities exchanged, the vessels used, and their intermediate ports of call.

The commercial exchange function has the greatest bearing on the location of most ports. They are best located when they serve the most productive parts of their hinterlands most efficiently. Assuming that the coastline is everywhere favourable, the actual location will relate to the cost of hauls to and from inland centres and those of ocean hauls.

Various solutions for a least-cost port situation have been put forward. Lösch[1] applied Snell's Law of Refraction. Assuming a cheap ocean freight rate F_0 and a costly land rate F_1, Fig. 70 shows that to ship a product most cheaply from A to B, the direct route AP_1B is discarded in favour of a route AP_2B; for the least-cost location will be where

$$F_0 \sin x - F_1 \sin y = 0$$

x and y being the angles of routes to the coastline.

As ocean freight rates increase, of course, the least-cost location will be nearer P_1 (as shown in II).

Urban Growth – Locating Factors

Fig. 72. *The urban sprawl of Bulli-Woollongong-Port Kembla along the coastland of New South Wales, between the Illawarra Range (IR) and the sea. Bulli's coal mines (C) can be seen in the foreground; beyond, near Lake Illawarra (L) are the steel and non-ferrous metal works at Port Kembla (PK), receiving metal ores through its harbour. Woollongong (W) is a residential area and business centre. The surfing beaches (R) provide recreational functions. Here we have urban growth about centres located in relation to local resources, on advantageous sites, and in a favourable position, south of the large metropolitan population of Sydney.*

Urban Form and Functions

The character of a town depends very much on its location and functions. Hexham, in Northumberland, still has the air of a strategic border town, close to the Tyne Gap through the Pennines. Its market functions are locally as important as ever—both as a regular commercial centre for the whole rural population and for farmers in a stock-rearing countryside.

Buxton has long been a health resort, based on the properties of hot springs. Its solid residential buildings, hotels, and places of entertainment, its gardens and spaciousness are in character with its role as a spa town, and make it very different in appearance from Midland manufacturing towns.

Fig. 73. (above) *One of Hexham's outdoor markets (there is a large livestock market nearby).*

Fig. 74 (below) *Buxton—a spa town in the Derbyshire Pennines.*

Fig. 75. Key to Fig. 72. Notice the Forest (F), burnt-out by bushfires, which can sweep into the suburbs of New South Wales coastal towns.

Ports: Location, Size, and Functions

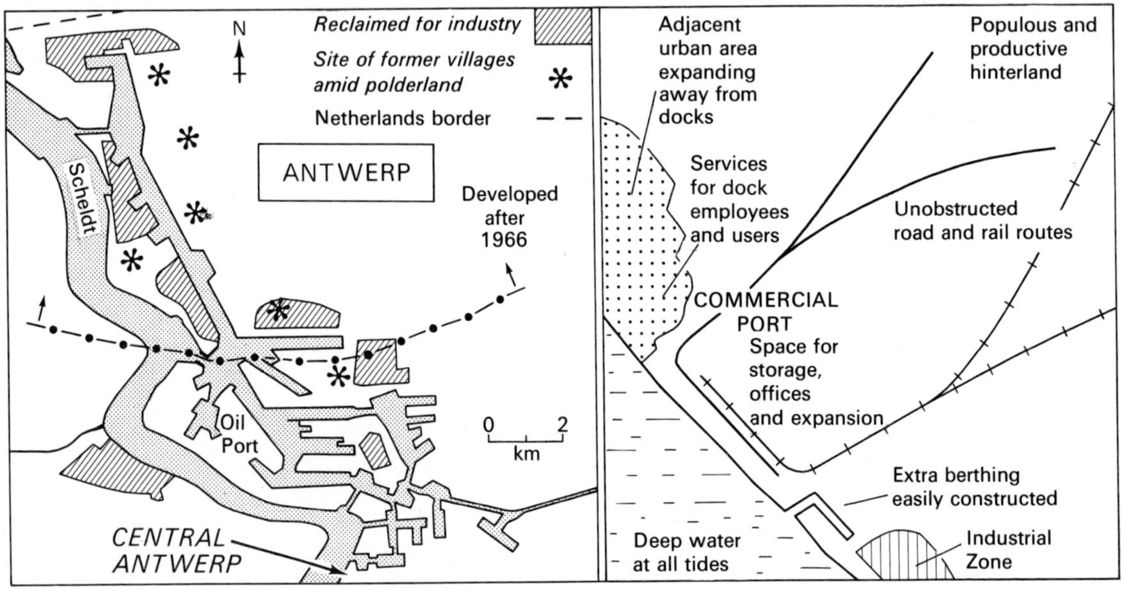

Fig. 76. *Recent developments of the docks and industrial sites at Antwerp have been down-river from the city centre and the original commercial port, taking up reclaimed land, and now stretch to the Netherlands border.*

Some of the features which allow a commercial port to flourish and expand are shown to the right. In many city-ports the docks become embedded in the growing urban area, which may come to include factories once sited near the docks and noxious industries formerly beyond residential areas.

Map labels:
- N
- Reclaimed for industry
- Site of former villages amid polderland
- Netherlands border
- ANTWERP
- Developed after 1966
- Scheldt
- Oil Port
- CENTRAL ANTWERP
- 0 2 km

Right diagram labels:
- Adjacent urban area expanding away from docks
- Populous and productive hinterland
- Services for dock employees and users
- Unobstructed road and rail routes
- COMMERCIAL PORT Space for storage, offices and expansion
- Extra berthing easily constructed
- Deep water at all tides
- Industrial Zone

Coastlines are seldom uniformly favourable for port construction, but sometimes locational advantages call for the development of an artificial port as near as possible to the most favourable least-cost location; such is Robert's Bank in southern British Columbia—a round artificial island stock-pile and port, which ships coal from Fernie to Japan and elsewhere.

In most cases, however, *site factors* have a strong influence on port location; particularly desirable are:

A waterfront able to berth many ships at once.

Deep water with little tidal fluctuation; freedom from silting (or, if not, easily dredged).

Clear approaches and easy access from the sea.

A sheltered roadstead, free from frequent fog.

Space for wharves and terminal installations.

Storage space, or access to container storage area.

Room for expansion and for allied urban growth.

Ready access to the docks for land transport.

Modern engineering can create locks to retain deep water, dredge approaches, extend jetties to deep water; so that even very unfavourable sites may be used where locational advantages are overwhelming. To maintain and extend Rotterdam and Europort amid the loose deltaic deposits of the Rhine involves great capital expense and technical achievement, but there is the incentive of productive hinterlands extending as far as northern Italy.

Ports and Other Functions

City-ports have, of course, the functions of any large urban area. Industrial functions are often related to those of the port. Some ports specialise in certain cargoes, and groups of industries may develop accordingly—imported oilseeds feeding crushing mills, food factories, and soap industries, for instance. Others have individual docks to supply particular industries; some, like oil terminals, feeding refineries and petro-chemical works, are often sited apart.

Fishing is an important function at certain ports with ready access to urban markets, and tends to generate local fish-preserving and manufacturing.

Industrial Functions:

Industries may be defined as *primary*, extractive industries, producing natural materials through mining or agriculture; *secondary* industries, transforming primary materials to useful commodities, generally by manufacture; and *tertiary* 'service' industries—transport, trade, administration etc.

Basic industries, which earn an income from sales to those outside the area in which they are situated, may be distinguished from *non-basic* industries.

Location of Industrial Functions

Primary industries, such as mining, are often precisely located. Frequently the industry is the main function of a town. Broken Hill, New South Wales, is primarily a mining town on the source of zinc, silver and lead ores, though it has other functions such as administration and retail trading (employing non-basic workers) which serve the mining community directly or indirectly.

Industrial Functions

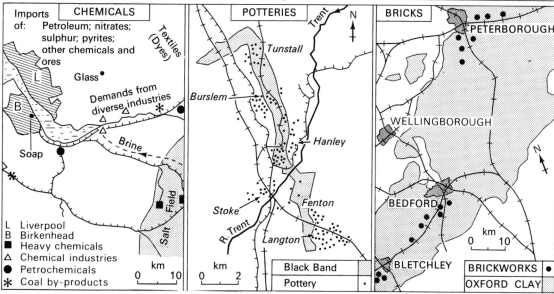

Fig. 77. In the chemical industries there are close relationships between the locations of raw materials (at source or point of import), of processing plants, and of the industries which use the chemical products.

Industrial inertia is seen in the North Staffordshire potteries where suitable coal and clays, outcropping in the Black Band group of Upper Coal Measures, were used for pottery. Later, Cornish clay, flint from France, and other bulky materials were imported, despite the inland location of these towns, where Wedgwood and others had transformed the art of pottery making.

By contrast, the majority of the country's bricks come from the resource-located works on the Oxford Clay belt.

In many mining areas, secondary industries employ large numbers. Mining towns on the coalfields of northern England usually acquired industrial functions at an early stage, as small engineering works, textile factories, and a host of non-basic industries grew up close to the source of power. Such 'mining towns' often came, later, to be termed 'textile', 'steel', or 'engineering' towns.

Industrial functions are often inter-related, and it may not be easy to distinguish the main ones. In large multifunctional cities, groups of industries are frequently clustered—oil refineries, petro-chemicals, plastics or synthetics firms, as well as those manufacturing goods using specific plastics or other synthetics. Transport manufacturing industries tend to attract satellite firms supplying parts and fittings.

Certain industries, of course, have special requirements. Chemical and metallurgical industries usually need large quantities of water, so that a riverside or lakeside site is advantageous. Others have particular human requirements; for instance, some confectionery firms find it preferable to employ middle-aged women working in groups in relative social harmony, so factories sited near residential suburbs more readily obtain suitable employees.

Many industries now choose the suburbs rather than the central urban areas, where even in old industrial towns, high land-rents induce industries to move out. For industries in suburbs, or along ring-roads, rents are cheaper, distribution easier, and urban markets are still at hand.

Whatever the reason for the initial industrial siting, as a town grows its functions increase. New industries may then be established to take advantage of its labour force and of products of existing industries. Its population may then increase further as employment opportunities attract outsiders.

The factors bearing on the location of manufacturing industries are complex and different for each group of industries. The optimum location depends on considerations of labour conditions, techniques used by particular firms, the nature and location of materials and markets, competition, and facts of transport and communications.

Power is now distributed through grid systems, and raw materials travel with increasing ease, so industrial location may hinge on market considerations; remember that the market for some industries (e.g. steel) may be other industrial firms.

Generally, if moving products to the customer is more costly than moving materials to the factory, it is as well to manufacture as near to the customer as possible—though customers are not always grouped together in a concentrated market area. If the market is widespread, industries serving it tend to be widespread (e.g. local building industries); but sometimes a large industry in a specific area serves national and international needs (e.g. car industries); here the cost, size, and mobility of the product come into consideration. Economic influences on industrial location, are so closely bound up with urban settlement that more detailed study is essential if we wish to examine the distribution of industrial populations.

Port and Outport

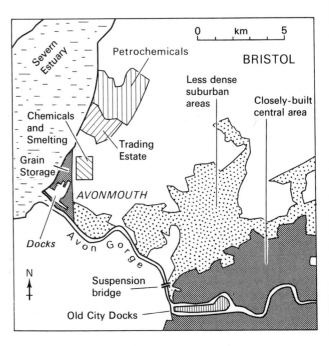

Fig. 78. Avonmouth and Severnside development.

Ships of limited draught reach the old city docks at Bristol at high water, via the Avon Gorge. Avonmouth has long been an active Severnside outport, and close by is a growing zone of industry and commerce, connected by trunk roads to the Midlands, South Wales, London, and the South West.

Fig. 79. The Clifton suspension bridge spans the Avon Gorge, whose exposures of Carboniferous Limestone can be seen on the right. This is low water: the entrance through the locks which retain deep-water in the old Bristol docks is to the right, foreground.

Fig. 80. At Avonmouth, Canadian grain is being transferred to a lighter bound for flour mills up-river, near Gloucester. Across the river are cranes used to unload aluminium; beyond are oil storage tanks.

Fig. 81. Hobart, capital city of Tasmania, seen from the east bank of the Derwent, with Mount Wellington to the right. The drowned valley of the lower Derwent, with its many inlets, gives deep water close inshore. The city has an excellent harbour, and there is almost no limit to which deep-water berthings could be extended along the estuary.

The site is superb, but the situation in relation to settlement and resources means that the harbour development and trade are only slight compared with mainland ports like Sydney and Melbourne. Hobart serves only a small island population, and its immediate hinterland is restricted.

Cultural, Recreational and Administrative Functions

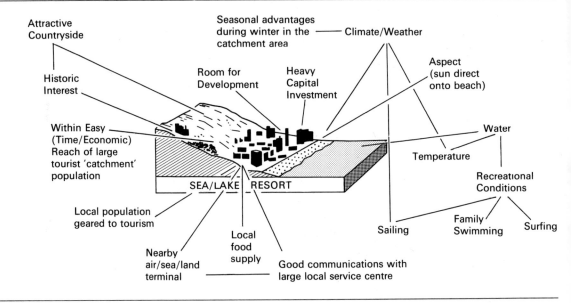

Fig. 82. *Physical and economic factors related to site and situation which affect the development of those resorts whose assets are primarily connected with a waterside location.*

Cultural and Religious Functions

Cultural and educational activities take place in any sizeable town. In some, education has become a dominant function, in the form of university, schools, or monastic centres of learning, and may, as at Oxford and Cambridge, remain of high importance. Educational functions may, however, yield to other functions in terms of basic employment of resident townsfolk—in Oxford to its transport industries, and in Cambridge, to a lesser extent, to electrical industries; also, in each of these cities, non-basic, service industries employ many thousands.

In some places religious functions may be pre-eminent, as in the Vatican city in Rome, the primate 'central place' at the head of other religious central places, descending through seats of archbishops and bishops, to lower-order places—the parishes. In Rome, if the Vatican is considered part of the whole urban area, this is but one function among many.

Few places retain cultural or religious activities as main functions. Mecca, in Saudi Arabia, is an exception, yet even this is a large trading centre, with Jeddah developed as its commercial port. Lourdes is a town connected fundamentally with pilgrimage, but also with secular tourism.

Tourist Functions and Resorts

The development of tourism has seen the growth of holiday areas and resort towns. Tourism is apt to be ignored as an industrial function; but today it is a widespread and most lucrative one which is of great economic importance to many countries. It has changed the character of numerous towns, created others, and led to continuous strips of semi-urban development along coastlines—in southern Spain, southern France, and northern Italy.

Some towns have, in the past, become fashionable centres, spa towns, for instance, like Bath and Harrogate, in England, and Vichy in France. But, with increasing ease of travel by land, sea and air, millions of people now visit coastal, lakeside, or scenic resorts at home and abroad, and make up a transient population much more numerous than the local one. Sunshine, water, and mountains have considerable locational holiday attraction. Figs. 82 and 83 show some of the geographical factors concerned.

Historic towns and sites are, of course, attractive to tourists: London, Edinburgh and Oxford rank tourism high among their other basic functions.

Administrative Functions

Again, any urban area will include forms of administration among its functions. Some towns, by virtue of supremacy as national or regional capitals have highly developed administrative functions, carried out from appropriately grand and complex buildings.

Certain Federal capitals, in their own Federal districts, have a special status and particular roles—Washington, Canberra and Brasilia for example. In these too, with time, other functions develop.

Man, the Land and Developing Patterns of Settlement

Fig. 83. Factors bearing on the development of resorts in mountainous country.

Fig. 84. Brasilia, the capital city of Brazil, lies nearly a thousand kilometres inland of Rio de Janeiro, the nearest city-port. It has been created, away from coastal commercial interests, with administration its main function, but also with the purpose of stimulating practical interest in the development of the interior of this vast country.

The deliberate planning of separate administrative and residential units is emphasised by the aircraft shape of the city, within a shallow basin on a climatically amenable part of the plateau. There is also considerable residential settlement in 'dormitory' areas beyond this central, planned city structure.

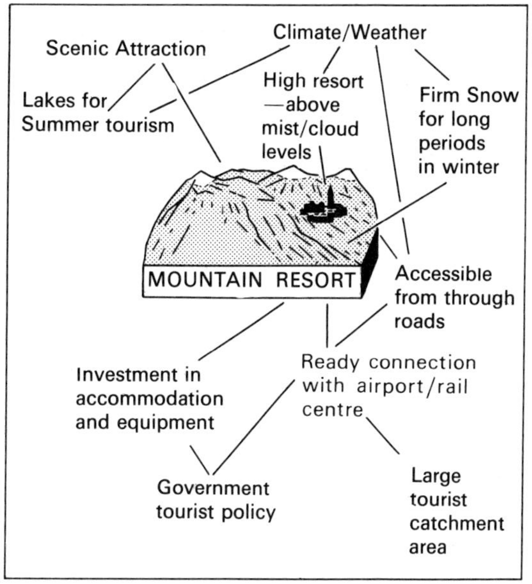

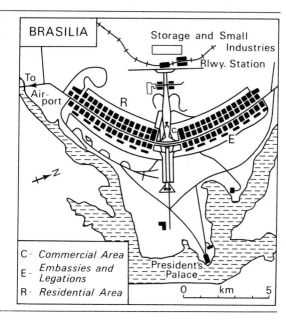

Washington is now part of a multifunctional urban agglomeration of some three million people. The functions of Canberra are still mostly connected with administrative, diplomatic and University activities, but recently others connected with national research projects have begun to encroach, and the tertiary industrial sector increases with the rapidly growing population. Brasilia is still in early stages of development, and fundamentally administrative and political, but rapidly increasing in size.

The nature and internal structure of metropolitan cities is discussed further in Chapter VIII.

Man and the Earth's Surface

The preceding pages have shown that thousands of millions of people occupy the earth's surface in communal groups, whose activities and arrangements vary greatly from place to place. The modes of life of peasant communities of the densely populated monsoon lowlands and the suburban dwellers in New York or Tokyo have little in common, and are subject to very different physical, social and economic influences.

There is a tendency to concentrate on geographical studies of life in the ever-expanding urban areas, and certainly these include a large proportion of the world's population—today, for instance, the majority of Australians are of 'suburbia' rather than of the 'outback'. But this should not distract us from examining the mode of life in areas of predominantly rural settlement, nor cause us to regard 'settlement' as synonymous with 'human clusters'. The sparsely populated, but agriculturally productive, steppes, prairies, and pampas are all essentially bound up with the maintenance of life and living standards in the urban areas. The gross overcrowding in Calcutta is related to the uncertainties of life, the vagaries of climate, and to various detrimental agricultural and social practices in the vast rural hinterland.

Nor should the numerically small groups of peoples be ignored. The wandering herdsmen of the savannahs may cause ecological changes over very large areas, affecting settlement in ways that are not immediately apparent—initiating erosion, changing run-off patterns, silting dams, and so, directly and indirectly, altering the landscape.

Developing Patterns

Organised responses to physical, social and economic pressure tend to result in recognisable patterns in human settlements. The fair distribution of good, poor, and indifferent land involves demarcation and boundaries, which may persist in the landscape. In urban areas, changing land values, overcrowding, social progress, and new techniques in transport and building may cause broadly similar patterns and zoning, recognisable in towns thousands of miles apart.

Such patterns, and their causes, form the main themes of the second part of this book.

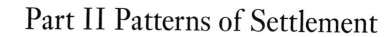

Part II Patterns of Settlement

Chapter V
Farms, Villages and Land-Use Patterns

Early Settlement

Fig. 85. Country in which colonists wish to settle and which presents a number of advantages and disadvantages. The map is based on the landscape shown in Fig. 1. The Table on page 65 shows weightings which represent priorities which might be attached to a number of local assets, and their distances from sites A and B. A preference for site A based on these considerations might be reversed if others, such as security, are important factors.

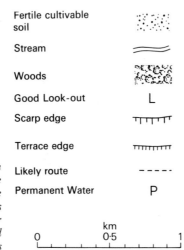

Fertile cultivable soil	
Stream	
Woods	
Good Look-out	L
Scarp edge	
Terrace edge	
Likely route	- - - - -
Permanent Water	P

km
0   0·5   1

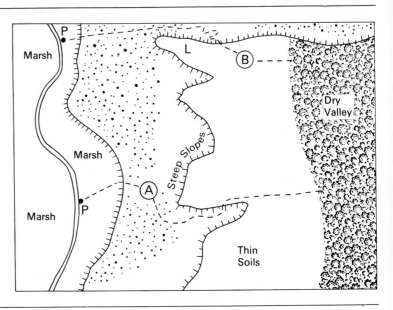

Initial Settlement—Factors and Choice

As men have moved about the earth's surface, choosing places to occupy, cultivate, and inhabit in small or large communities, they have been subject to innumerable influences and pressures. As thinking beings, able to consider alternatives, they have been moved to seek territory which could provide their various needs—available water, a dry site for habitation, land with fertile soils and easy to clear, and a supply of wood. They have hoped to enjoy such assets free from competition from neighbouring groups. Where alternative sites were available for occupation, many whose first choice proved unsuitable must have moved on to clear and settle other land.

In some cases a particular advantage would seem to outweigh all others, perhaps nearness to water or the need to occupy a defensive site (see Fig. 1). But often a combination of advantageous factors would

be weighed together, consciously or unconsciously, and new settlement made accordingly.

We may use such a situation, therefore, to demonstrate how such influential factors might operate to influence choice of site[2]. Taking the example already considered in Fig. 1, we can mark on a plan of the area watering points (P); rich land on a river terrace; a flood-plain, difficult to cross; lowland beneath a scarp, a possible routeway for hostile folk; a dip-slope with poor soils, and a sheltered dry valley, which has the only thick woodland.

Two possible sites would seem likely. A, with the advantages of nearness to the best cultivable land and to a good watering point, but far from sources of fuel and good timber, and with possible exposure to hostile groups; and B, with the advantages of security and nearness to fuel and timber, but far from a reliable watering point and rich soils.

If we consider the four resources, water, good cultivable land, fuel, and timber, we may allocate to each a weighting (1–10) according to their desir-

ability and how frequently they are needed. We may then measure the distance of each from the possible sites A and B. When the weighting (W) is multiplied by the distance (d) for each of the four resources and the products added, the site with the lowest total would appear to be the most advantageous. Weighting is a personal decision; but those figures used in the table shown indicate that A would be preferable to B. Others, however, might view the relative advantages differently, and, in any case, an element of chance is likely in such decision-making.

Patterns of Settlement

Despite the elements of chance involved, in time, most occupied landscapes bear recognisable *patterns* of settlement; patterns which vary with the topography and with the customs and technological abilities of the men themselves. Of course, increasing pressure of population, or economic circumstances, may cause changes in these patterns.

Site	Resource	Distance from Resource d (km)	Weighting W (max 10)	dW
A	Water	0·4	8	3·2
	Soil	0·0	6	0·0
	Fuel	1·7	4	6·8
	Timber	1·7	2	3·4
			Total	13·4
B	Water	1·2	8	9·6
	Soil	0·5	6	3·0
	Fuel	0·3	4	1·2
	Timber	0·3	2	0·6
			Total	14·4

Patterns Evolve

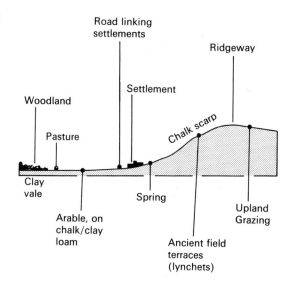

Fig. 86. *Elements of regularity which appeared in the settlement of the escarpments of southern Britain and the gradual occupation of the adjoining vales.*

Nevertheless, we frequently recognise spatial regularities in the forms of both simple and complex human settlements, either as relics of the past or as responses to present conditions. In Britain numerous characteristic historic patterns may be recognised in the landscape, some from pre-Christian settlement, many from the earliest development of Christian parishes, and others resulting from the competitive growth of hamlets, villages and towns through the centuries. Even within the complex modern city, typical patterns have evolved and are evolving.

Early Rural Settlement in Britain

There is much visible evidence of late Stone Age and Bronze Age settlement in southern Britain, especially in the burial mounds and stone circles on those hills which, being less heavily wooded than the adjoining lowlands, were easier to clear and occupy. Later, but still hundreds of years before the Roman occupation, Celtic peoples, using iron implements, created field systems on hills and downs in the south and south-west. Their small broad fields with low embankments (lynchets) are still visible under the turf on chalk downlands. Little remains of the isolated upland farms and hamlets of the early Bronze Age people, but in troubled times they constructed earthworks and forts on the hills, and these are still impressive landscape features.

These hardly represent a 'pattern' of settlement, but a regularity persisted in their choice of sites and certain linking roads follow a common alignment visible today—notably tracks or 'ridgeways' running along the summits of chalk escarpments (Fig. 91).

Shortly before the Roman invasions, ploughs with 'mould boards', which turned the heavy soils, were introduced and enabled arable farming to be extended onto the lowlands. Here, and at the junctions of downs and vales, a patterned distribution of various qualities of land began to evolve.

The strategically sited camps and towns of Roman Britain, together with the accompanying network of roads, did not generally relate to this earlier settlement. Although many Roman sites are still occupied by large towns, and though some of the modern roads follow a Roman alignment, the Romans left no overall patterns of rural settlement on the broad countryside.

Settlement Patterns Evolve

At the foot of the chalk escarpments ground-water maintains a number of permanent streams. Early settlements sited close to these sources of water could use relatively dry sites at the foot of the scarp, farm the nearby chalk-clay loams, cut into the woodlands in the vale beyond, and graze animals on the shortgrass chalkland turf above.

Such choice of site was good, even excluding water as a determining consideration, for on a 'weighted factor' basis the location may be seen to be one which minimises the 'costs' and efforts of daily activities of a small agricultural community (see p. 72).

Escarpment Parishes

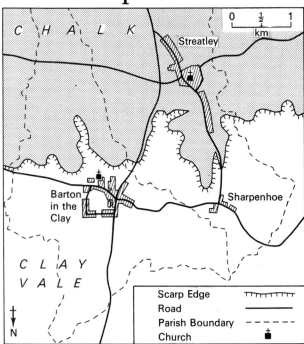

Fig. 88. Notice the long parishes running back from the clay vale onto the chalk and down the dip-slope, and also the lines of the roads above and below the scarp. Barton, like Harlington and Pirton, also in the vale a few kilometres west and east of it, is, typically, the main parish settlement; but in the parish containing the route centre of Streatley, the church is above, while Sharpenhoe beneath is a small hamlet.

Fig. 87. Streatley in south Bedfordshire, where the ancient road up the spur of the chalk met tracks following the top of the escarpment. The village has expanded away from the old centre about the church, along the line of the old roads. The main Luton–Bedford road is seen to the left. Notice the beech woodlands on the steep sides of the dry valleys extending back into the scarp.

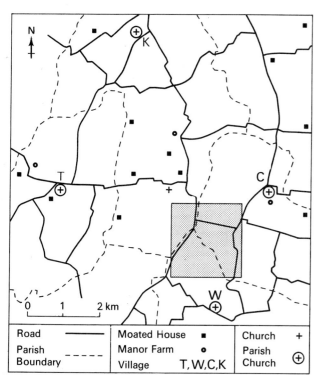

Fig. 89. Parishes on the Midland lowlands, in north Bedfordshire. Notice the spacing of the villages (T–Thurleigh; K–Keysoe; C–Colmworth; W–Wilden). This has long been a landscape of large farms. Most of the moated homesteads belonged to small feudal landowners; not all have survived as farms (but see Fig. 130). Landscape features of the stippled inset may be seen in Fig. 90.

Figs. 87 and 90, in the south and north of a small Midland county, respectively, typify the diversity so often found in the relief, soils, and settlement patterns in the English landscape within a relatively short distance. Between the two, in fact, lies a Greensand outcrop with quite different settlement patterns: there are many large estates and formal parks on its relatively infertile soils.

Fig. 90. A landscape of enclosure in north Bedfordshire, with large dispersed farmsteads. Notice the angular pattern of the roads in response to ancient boundaries, and the common path of the small stream, field limits and parish boundary (dotted line), bottom right.

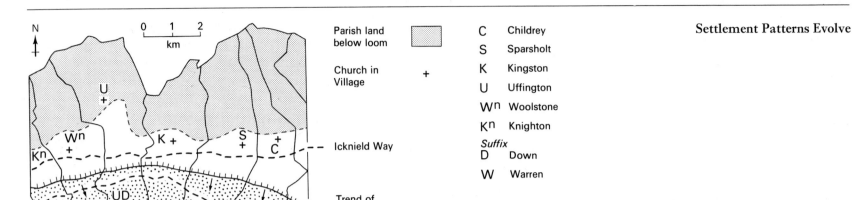

Legend:

Parish land below loom

Church in Village +

Icknield Way

Trend of Scarp (ca. 220 m)

Dip Slope

Ridgeway

Parish boundary

C Childrey
S Sparsholt
K Kingston
U Uffington
Wn Woolstone
Kn Knighton

Suffix
D Down
W Warren

PARISHES WEST OF WANTAGE

Fig. 91. These long parishes immediately west of Wantage, Berkshire, extend from the dip-slope of the chalk down onto the White Horse Vale. Notice the central position of most of these villages, close to the spring-line, and also the alignments of the ancient ways; the Icknield Way is still in use as a modern road.

The Chalklands

When Christianity was re-established and churches built, the parish boundaries on and adjacent to the chalklands closely followed the bounds of earlier settlements. They extended from the vale to the top of the escarpment and included common land on the dip-slope, which usually bore the name of the parish below; a pattern which can be seen today (Fig. 91).

The Midland Lowland

As Saxon groups slowly colonised the Midland lowlands, they too sought resources similar to those described above. They included land suitable for ploughing, pasture and common grazing as they cleared outward from the centre of settlement (p. 20).

Choice of site would have been influenced by considerations of drainage and defence. Suitable distance could be maintained from neighbouring groups of people, while allowing sufficient land to support each expanding settlement.

As new settlers arrived, however, and older settlements 'hived off' their excess population, the countryside became more and more closely occupied. The establishment of churches, and tributary areas defined by parish boundaries, perpetuated the patterns of these early settlements, with their 'territories' adjoining one another. Here, on the lowlands, the villages tended to be centrally located, though there were numerous variations, related to differences of soils and minor relief features. Many of these parish boundaries have since been realigned.

Soil Variations and Land-Use Patterns

Varying soil conditions have always strongly influenced the patterns of settlement. Where broad rivers crossed lowlands, early settlements were often sited relatively close to a river and, making use of gravel terraces, spaced a mile or so apart along the bank. Thus their holdings extended back in a strip from the river to include moist alluvial meadowland, better drained arable soils, and drier grazing land beyond; a pattern resembling that of the colonial French settlements in the St. Lawrence valley (p. 21).

In modern Kenya, we see similar influences of relief, soils, and drainage conditions on patterns of settlements created by re-distribution of agricultural land in the Highlands north of Nairobi (p. 70).

Here volcanic materials with fertile soils are deeply dissected by parallel streams running from a main watershed. Land held by Kikuyu families had become small, scattered units; so a new arrangement came about, allowing each family the same amount of land, but in a continuous consolidated unit.

As Fig. 94 shows, each new holding runs from ridge-top to valley floor. The homesteads are high on the slopes, often along a road leading to a re-sited village. The slopes are terraced and the variations in soils down-slope are mirrored by variations in crops grown at the various levels (Fig. 95). Thus a more or less regular pattern of equal distribution is achieved.

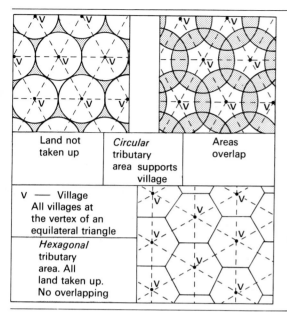

| Land not taken up | *Circular* tributary area supports village | Areas overlap |

V — Village
All villages at the vertex of an equilateral triangle
Hexagonal tributary area. All land taken up. No overlapping

Settlements and Tributary Areas

Fig. 92. Regularly spaced villages on a plain, where physical and agricultural conditions are uniform. It is seen that the hexagon is the most efficient areal shape which will 'pack' without leaving spaces or overlapping, while giving good access to the central village from all parts of the tributary area.

Fig. 93. Village V_2, like the other villages, draws custom from and serves the hamlets H; these hamlets, however, share their custom with two other villages equidistant from them. Notice the relationship between the villages V_1—V_2 and the settlement T, and see page 100. Consider the role of T, and where similar settlements would be found.

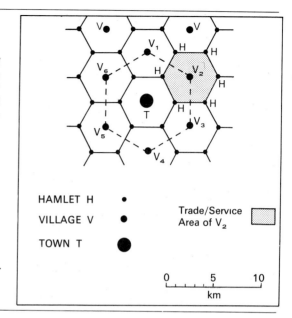

HAMLET H   •
VILLAGE V   •
TOWN T   ●

Trade/Service Area of V_2

0   5   10
km

Small Settlements—Patterns of Distribution

So far we have examined relationships between men and the physical landscape—scarps, ridges, soil variations, water supplies. But the evolution of settlement patterns also involves complex sets of relationships between men and men.

Let us once again assume, for simplicity, that peoples with limited technological advantages are colonising a uniform plain. Their simple settlements would tend to be grouped so that each had an adequate 'tributary area' to support them. Each would be spaced a few miles from neighbouring settlements. There would be a maximum population which the resources of this tributary area could support before some migrated to colonise new territory. As more and more village groups form, the most likely pattern would be that where each settlement holds land equally accessible from its centre, and the relative location of each is at the vertex of an equi-

lateral triangle (Fig. 92). This arrangement would either leave some land not taken up, or the 'tributary areas' would overlap; but a tributary area of hexagonal shape allows the greatest density of settlement with the shortest distance from each central place to the edge of its territory.

We are, of course, considering hypothetical patterns in uniform environmental conditions. But the use of simple models and empirical studies does enable us to recognise similar patterns in an actual landscape; or we may be led to consider why such patterns do *not* appear where we would expect them; or perhaps we may recognise them but realise that they are masked by other settlement features. In each case we have gained by establishing a useful theoretical model in our search for spatial order.

Market Functions: Central Places

In a closely settled landscape with many small self-supporting hamlets (H), it is likely that, through enterprise or locational advantage, the occasional

hamlet begins to offer surplus produce for sale and comes to establish itself as a small trading centre with market functions. An increase in functions is usually accompanied by an increase in population, and so small market villages (V) evolve.

But these, too, must have sufficient customers from a tributary area if they are to flourish, and will compete with other villages for custom. Assuming travel is with pack animals over rough roads, four kilometres to market and four back would be a reasonable distance to travel regularly from hamlet to village. With hamlets located at the vertices of equilateral triangles, we see that a hexagonal pattern is likely, with service villages central to six hamlets (as V_2 in Fig. 92) and competing for their custom with other village central places, themselves part of a hexagonal pattern of equal ranking places.

The German geographer W. Christaller[3] recognised the principle of hexagonal settlement patterns, based on observations of retail/service business and market areas in southern Germany (p. 100).

69

Settlement Patterns on Ridges and Valleys

Fig. 94. *Ridge and vale country north of Nairobi, with a variety of crops on family holdings aligned as part of a resettlement plan. Maize cobs lie on the clearing in the foreground, outside houses sited similarly to those across the valley.*

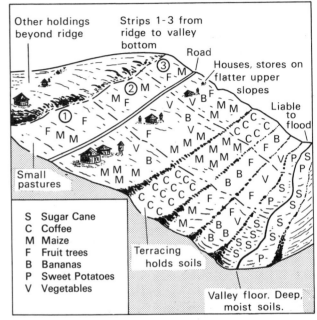

Other holdings beyond ridge

Strips 1-3 from ridge to valley bottom

Road

Houses, stores on flatter upper slopes

Liable to flood

Small pastures

Terracing holds soils

Valley floor. Deep, moist soils.

S Sugar Cane
C Coffee
M Maize
F Fruit trees
B Bananas
P Sweet Potatoes
V Vegetables

Fig. 95. *A diagrammatic view of land-use on holdings similar to those seen in Fig. 93.*

The Government policy of consolidating fragments of land once scattered about these steep hillsides has enabled each family group to build its houses and small stores on the upper slopes of the valley, where a new linking path or road may run, and to farm a continuous strip of land from the hill-top to valley-floor.

As can be seen, each family plants a variety of subsistence and cash crops, and maize, bananas, coffee and fruit trees occupy various levels. In some cases, cattle are grazed close to the settlement and poultry kept about the homestead. The overall settlement pattern is due to planning; the individual land-use patterns still respond to relief, soils, and drainage.

Fig. 96. The flat, fertile Indo-Gangetic plains of northern India, some fifty kilometres north-west of Delhi. The settlement pattern is of food crops and sugar-cane grown by farmers who live in small, compact villages about larger townships, like that in the foreground. Routes converge on these market towns; as their alignment and the relative positions of ponds (tanks), rough land fringing the settlements, and the field boundaries indicate, neither towns nor villages have expanded greatly in recent times, despite the overall population growth. Surplus population of the rural districts tends to move to the large towns and thence to the cities (p. 49).

Figure 97

von THUNEN'S ISOLATED STATE

[Early 19th C Conditions]

All farmers wish to maximise profits

Uniform Plain

Horse-drawn, transport

Single Central City (Sole Market)

Land-Use can be adjusted to market needs

Farm *

Zone (—)

Each farmer considers yields per unit area.
Bulk of products
Distance from market
Market prices

Net return per unit area: beyond *a*, 2>1; beyond *b*, 3>2; and so on.

Extensive grazing

three-field system

Less intensive

Crop farming; fallow; pasture

Wood in great demand

River allows speedier, less costly transport

6 | 5 | 4 | |3|2|1| CITY
e | d | | c b a

Land-Use Zones

1 Market gardening Dairying
2 Firewood/lumber
3 Intensive arable
4 Arable/Long Ley
5 Three-Field Arable
6 Grazing

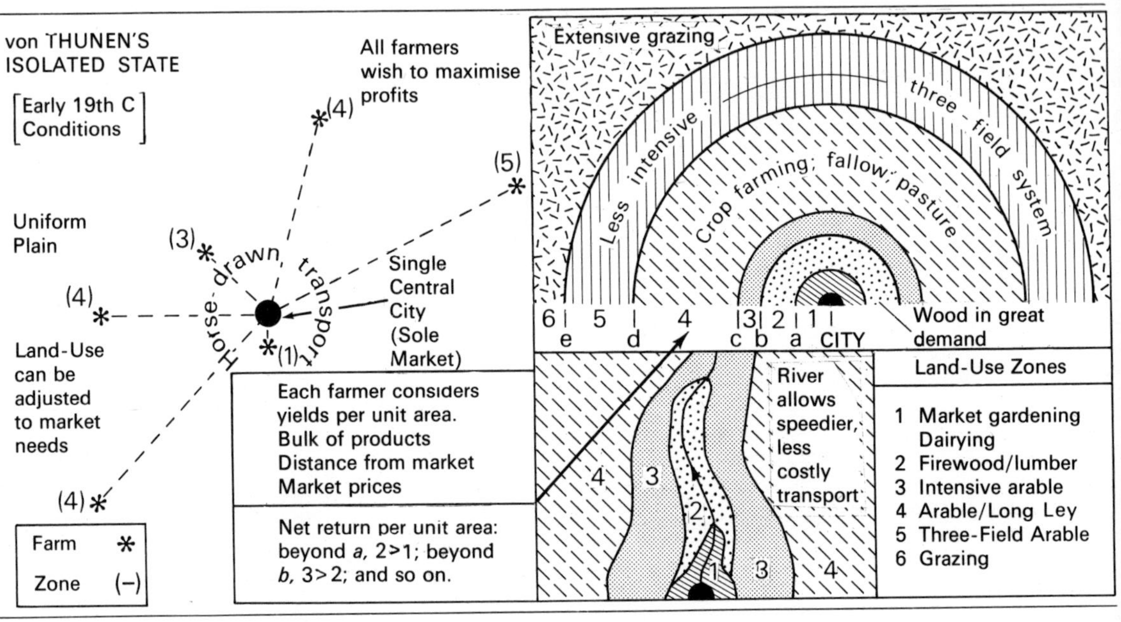

Fig. 97. Patterns of land-use changing with distance from a single urban market, as expounded by J. H. von Thünen. The conditions are of uniform fertility and apply to his own times—when timber was much in demand, for fuel and building, and was, of course, a bulky material incurring high transport cost.

These results of his analyses are put forward simply to stress that such facts as yield per unit acre, production costs, crop-bulk, transport rates, distance from market, and market prices tend to create zoning in types of agricultural land-use. It reflects a substitution of products as distance from market increases, and the return per unit area from one form of land-use falls to a point where it is more profitable to produce another (perhaps less bulky) commodity. Likely effects of cheap transport by water are shown below.

Rural Settlements: Patterns of Adjoining Land-use

In simple rural settlements depending on animal transport a recognisable zoning of land-use has tended to develop about each farmstead, hamlet, and village.

An early analysis of land-use patterns in north-eastern Europe was made by J. H. von Thünen[4], who managed an estate near Rostock. He observed certain areal relationships between agricultural activities and the accounts he was responsible for, and in 1826 published a book which analysed these relationships. He was interested in the prices of agricultural products, the ways in which their variations could be related to patterns of land-use, and how types of produce and farming systems competed for the use and development of particular areas.

von Thünen postulated an 'isolated state', in which one city was surrounded by arable land with uniform physical conditions. All surplus produce had to be sold in the city, and each farmer bore transport costs (of horse-drawn vehicles) which varied with distance. Each farmer wished to obtain the highest net return from each specified piece of land and was ready to put it to the most profitable use.

von Thünen considered the monetary return over and above the expenses incurred by adopting the various forms of agriculture—that is the net return from unit land area under a particular form of agricultural use, such as market gardening, wheat growing, or potato cultivation. As a result he obtained, theoretically, the 'ideal arrangement', whereby the various types of land-use occupied a series of concentric zones about the city (Fig. 97).

Land-Use Zones about a Farmstead

In practice, of course, it is not likely that there would be uniform physical conditions; and not all farmers strive after the optimum return. But let us consider an individual farmer who *is* capable of the finest judgment, and aims to maximise his return for the effort he puts in. He is, of course, aware of the law of diminishing returns; that is, if any extra input results in a smaller additional return from a particular activity, he will re-direct that input to obtain a maximum return from another form of land-use on another part of his land.

Distance and Zoning

The time of travel to and from the fields is part of the farmer's input. Cultivating lands further from the farm entails more travel time, so that a greater total input is needed to obtain from them a return similar to that from land near the farm. A farmer may be able to cut the cost of using the distant land by putting it to a less intensive form of land-use.

In dairy farming, which involves bringing in animals for milking (or carrying in the produce) and supplying feed, the costs per unit area increase rapidly with distance from the farm buildings. The 'friction of distance' is great, and the return to the farmer is higher per unit of land nearer the centre.

Patterns and Returns from the Land

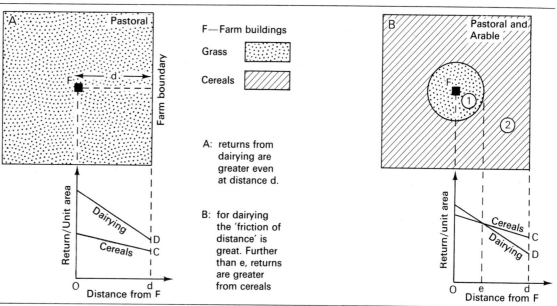

Fig. 98. Patterns resulting from a rational response to returns from different forms of land-use (assuming uniform relief, soils, and micro-climatic conditions).

In A the return from dairy farming is so great that the farm is entirely pastoral land. In B, with higher market prices for cereals, and as the costs of dairying increase considerably with distance, at a distance e from the farmstead a higher return is obtained if cereals are grown; so that, theoretically, the land-use pattern should appear as in plan B.

A: returns from dairying are greater even at distance d.

B: for dairying the 'friction of distance' is great. Further than e, returns are greater from cereals

With arable crops, however, it matters less whether they are grown near the centre or further off, for they require less regular attention, and so the return per unit area falls less rapidly with distance.

Today, woodland needs infrequent attention, but yields valuable timber; so it may be profitable to leave outer parts of the holding under woodland.

The overall result is zoning about the centre, the form of which varies with the nature of the agricultural activities and the net income per unit area the farmer is likely to receive.

Market Prices and Zoning

Zoning will, of course, vary with outside economic factors and fluctuating market prices; so that, theoretically, the zones should be adjusted from time to time. But changing from one form of agriculture to another is usually a long-term process, and the farmer may be unable, or unwilling, to change forms of land-use with such fluctuations.

In Fig. 98A dairy farming would give the greatest return over most of the area, and this may well be simply a 'dairy farm'. In Fig. 98B cereals are fetching a higher price and bring a greater return; so that, while land near the farm is grazed by dairy cattle (zone 1), cereals pay better in zone 2.

Modifying Factors

The variations of relief, climate, and soils influence the land-use patterns. If natural conditions need modifying by levelling, draining, or adding fertiliser, the additional cost will affect zoning'.

Many other factors may add to, or subtract from, the farmer's input, and so increase or lessen his returns. There may be subsidies for a particular form of land-use; there are ever-changing costs of seed and stock, fertilisers, pesticides, irrigation, machinery (purchase or hire), and variations in outside labour costs—all of which affect calculations. Besides these, returns will fluctuate with improve-

ments in external transport facilities, and with changing methods of packing and distribution. For instance, small-bulk produce per unit value can generally bear the cost of transportation better than more bulky produce. Then there will be changes in the seasonal combinations of crops in order to maintain fertility of the land.

The result is that, though there may be recognisable zones of land-use in response to return-distance factors, they are generally modified by a host of other facts and circumstances. In modern temperate mixed farming it is indeed difficult to find clear examples of such zoning: modern forms of transport lessen the 'friction of distance' and, in intensive commercial agriculture, the proportion of internal 'travel costs' to total income is relatively small.

Clear zoning is usually much more apparent in peasant farming and about relatively simple forms of village settlement, and is still easy to identify in many parts of the Mediterranean lands.

Land-Use about a Village

Fig. 99. *Episkopi in southern Cyprus; the minaret denotes the centre of this Turkish-Cypriot settlement. Fruit trees, irrigated vegetable plots, and vines grow among the houses and close to the village, and vegetables and other field crops are cultivated beneath the olives. All can be regularly tended within a short distance of the household.*

Beyond this sheep graze on rougher ground, which extends outwards between old olives towards bare limestone 'pavements' further west.

Fig. 100. Ayios Ambrosios, among the limestone hills south of the Troodos mountains in Cyprus. Here are some of the principal vineyards of the country. The cultivators live in compact villages, rather than in dispersed farms.

Again the brighter green indicates the zone of vegetables and fruit trees close to the village. Further from the village the hillsides in all directions are covered with vines, which need a great deal of attention, but involve periodic work and not daily labour through the year.

Land-Use Zones

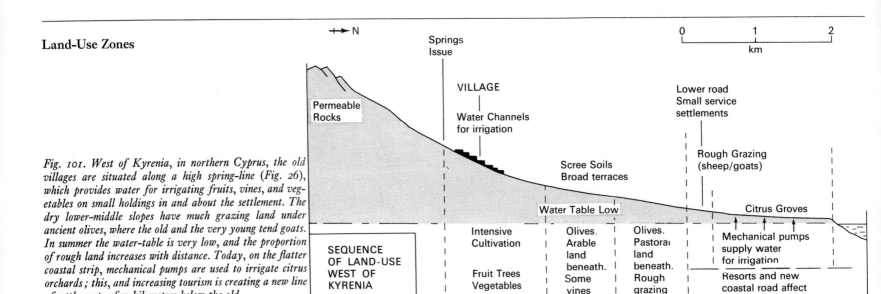

Fig. 101. West of Kyrenia, in northern Cyprus, the old villages are situated along a high spring-line (Fig. 26), which provides water for irrigating fruits, vines, and vegetables on small holdings in and about the settlement. The dry lower-middle slopes have much grazing land under ancient olives, where the old and the very young tend goats. In summer the water-table is very low, and the proportion of rough land increases with distance. Today, on the flatter coastal strip, mechanical pumps are used to irrigate citrus orchards; this, and increasing tourism is creating a new line of settlement a few kilometres below the old.

The Village Land-Use Patterns

In many Mediterranean countries the nucleated settlements are, in effect, 'agro-settlements': villages from which workers move out to the nearby cultivated land. Here there is often a clear relationship between distance from the village and land-use.

Near the villages are small fields, bounded by stone walls or prickly pear hedges, in which are grown vegetables, fruit trees, such as citrus, almonds, and mulberries, and 'household' vines. This is an inner zone of intensive cultivation of land held by various members of the community, with fruit and vines grown in courtyards among the houses, and even on roof-tops. The soil is not necessarily of high quality, and indeed in some places is brought from elsewhere, in the way that terra rossa is supplied to the small, sunken fields in some parts of Malta.

Beyond, are arable lands with a relatively high proportion of olives and carob trees, sometimes with a grain crop, or vines, growing beneath—each commodity calling for much labour at certain times of the year. The intensity of the grain cultivation varies with the soils and climate. If, in marginal conditions, it is found that a great input of labour is needed, more, than for an equivalent area of vines and olives, the latter will tend to occupy an outer zone.

Still further from the settlement, close cultivation gives way to a more open landscape, with more and more fields left fallow for long periods, and with rough grazing occupying most of the countryside between the cultivated areas about the villages.

Whatever the land-use, Mediterranean 'agro-settlements' almost always show a zoned distribution of crops, based on labour requirements and distance—though mechanisation blurs the pattern, and motor-scooters carry workers to cultivate fertile land far from the village.

Zoning Tendencies—Regional Differences

In the English lowlands, with their close distribution of villages, many parts of the rural parishes now have single large farms or farm clusters, each with their own arrangements of fields and rotation systems. This, of course, disturbs any overall zoning about the village, though there may still be a noticeable, if blurred, pattern of land-use about certain villages. There is rarely a single market, nor homogeneous surface, and transport costs have declined in relation to other agricultural costs—all of which make for complex combinations of land-use.

In some countries, close agricultural occupation is made up mainly of small holdings, as we have seen in Uganda, where these yield both subsistence foods and cash crops such as cotton, coffee and groundnuts. Yet these small holdings do, in fact, tend to show zones of cultivation. Crops like coffee, which need much attention are usually near the homestead, with maize or cassava plots beyond, giving way to land periodically burnt over for rough pasture. Here, as Figs. 30 and 32 show, villages and small towns have market functions and provide rural services.

Rural-Urban Fringes

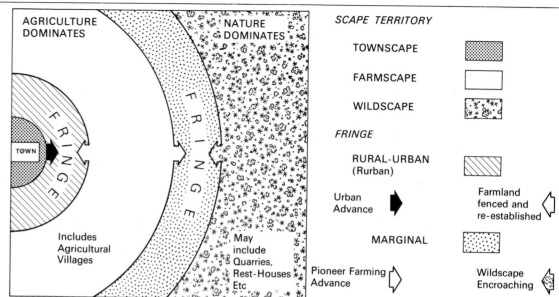

Fig. 102. *A general model showing the relationships between three 'scapes' and the fringe territories between them. A simple model such as this helps to clarify thoughts about more complex landscapes in the field, and is an aid to the interpretation of Land Utilisation Maps, where many categories of land-use are seen to be intermingled.*

Notice the use of the term 'dominate'. The territories are not completely urban, or farmland, or 'wild', and may include other forms of land-use. The arrows indicate that advances and retreats into the fringe areas occur. Planning aims to eliminate such fringes, which are usually unsatisfactory zones of 'conflict'.

(Based on a model put forward by Miss Alice Coleman[5]).

Other Rural Patterns

There are, of course, patterns of land-use and settlement which have not slowly evolved and established zoning on a distance/time/cost basis (see p. 29). Fig. 103 shows part of the Murrumbidgee Irrigation area in southern New South Wales, where, from 1906 onwards, planning has established the form of the rural settlement about specially sited nuclei.

Here we see a planned zoning which, initially, aimed at developing concentric belts about these compact settlement centres; small two-acre blocks for urban workers; fruit/vegetable blocks of some five to twenty acres near the towns, where there are better soils, and farms are perennially provided with water, and an outer zone of larger farms with dairying and fodder crops, based on partial irrigation.

With time, this system was modified as, amongst other factors, lucerne crops were not well suited by the water conditions in the outlying areas, nor by the effects of irrigation on these particular soils. Dairy-

ing was therefore replaced by a long rotation of rice with pasture for fat lambs. This generally meant an increase in the size of the farms in this outer belt.

In this case, the distance factor was related not only to time but to difficulties of supplying gravity-fed water, and soil variations were important considerations, affecting both the initial layout and later modifications. The result, however, was to establish recognisable patterns in the landscape.

Rural/Urban Transition

A rural settlement may in time acquire more functions and offer more services; but, like many of the nucleated towns in southern Italy, it may remain rural rather than urban in character.

In many cases it is very difficult to distinguish between 'rural' and 'urban' settlements, but the essential distinctions must be in functions rather than in size. Administrative, social and cultural functions, as well as those of commerce and manu-

facturing, are involved in the development of an urban settlement.

There is not necessarily any regular progression from village to rural township to urban status, even under the uniform physical conditions which tend to result in the regular spacing and ordering of central places noted by Christaller and others; but, of course, a central position, a strategic position, or location at a concentration of routes caused by physical barriers, tends to create strong commercial functions, and stimulate the development of retailing and local industries.

Settlement maps clearly indicate relationships between urbanisation and density of communications. So, before turning to facts of urban location and the spacing of towns, it is as well to consider the influences of available forms of transport, and how particular patterns of communication may evolve.

The close inter-relationships between patterns of settlement and route links and networks are considered on pp. 89-95.

Planned Settlement – Land-Use Variations

Fig. 103. Leeton, inland in New South Wales, about 600 km south-west of Sydney, was established to serve an agricultural countryside in the Murrumbidgee Irrigation Area. The regularities of its lay-out and of the land itself are obvious. Here small blocks produce vegetables and fruit, a form of land-use which continues outwards on the better, more regularly irrigated soils. Fruit and vegetable canneries can be seen to the right.

Further out, the holdings are much larger and grow rice in long-rotation with pastures, which support fat lambs. Leeton is the recipient of the grain, wool, and meat from settlement dispersed over a wide area and acts as the business, retail, and recreational centre. The larger buildings of the shops, hotels, and church can be seen near the centre of the town, and the sports oval beyond.

Fig. 104. Turvey in Bedfordshire, whose church, overlooking the river Ouse, contains the structure of its Saxon predecessor, built in 980. The heart of the old settlement was near the bridge-head and mill (just off the picture to the left).

It is tempting to see the village still as a small 'rural central place' and of the countryside. But much was built in the mid-nineteenth century, even stone buildings of its attractive main street, when the school was built and the church extensively restored. Today, local farms are embedded in housing, some inter-War, some of the 'fifties, and a small modern estate.

Lying on the main road from Northampton (20 km) to Bedford (13 km), its functions as a commuter settlement for each. Bedford is its main shopping centre (Fig. 153); it has four general stores for convenience goods, and three large inns.

Chapter VI
Transport Systems and Route Networks

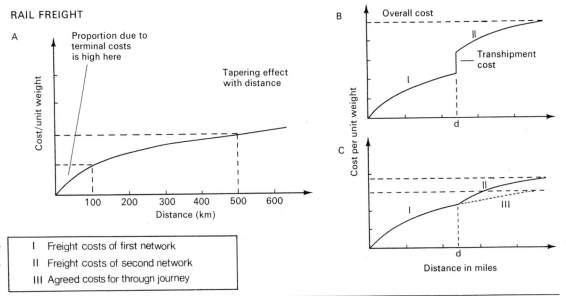

RAIL FREIGHT

A — Cost/unit weight vs Distance (km)
Proportion due to terminal costs is high here
Tapering effect with distance
100 200 300 400 500 600
Distance (km)

B — Cost per unit weight vs d
Overall cost
Transhipment cost
I II

C — Cost per unit weight vs d
II
I
III
Distance in miles

I   Freight costs of first network
II Freight costs of second network
III Agreed costs for through journey

Fig. 105. The rates charged for freight movements are closely connected with the efficiency of the system. A shows that high terminal costs (those of documentation, storage, depreciation of capital assets, etc.) make the cost per mile very high for short journeys. B shows how transhipment from one rail network to another adds to the cost, with new terminal expenses creating another steep rise beyond d. *C shows the advantages of the through-journey, avoiding actual transhipment (agreements for bogey changes, etc.), with (I-II) and without (I-III) new terminal costs at* d.

Transport Systems and Communication Patterns

Observe any settled landscape from the air, or study settlement on a map of the order of R.F. 1 : 200 000, and one is struck by the patterns of routeways that are seen radiating from central places; one may see the significance of those linking one 'web' with another, and the lines of the trunk roads, railways, or canals cutting across these webs and networks. Here and there an airfield is a reminder of the invisible flight-patterns at various altitudes.

The different forms of transport, whose various advantages and disadvantages are described below, together with their appropriate routeways, combine to form a number of *transport systems* serving the needs of the inhabitants of the area and, extending beyond this settled landscape, linking them with peoples and resources elsewhere. Such systems may be made up of different forms of transport.

The Efficiency of a Transport System

An efficient transport system, even with different vehicles and a variety of routeways, should be able to move passengers and small consignments rapidly, over short and long journeys, to any destination within its limits; move bulk consignments cheaply; deal with specialised goods, such as perishable foodstuffs, or liquids, and cope with periodic demands, such as commuter rush-hours, or movements of seasonal agricultural produce.

Costs

In all these operations costs should be kept to a minimum. Among the costs which may be involved in moving a consignment from X to Y are:

Loading Costs : these vary with the ease of handling the consignment, and the numbers of employees and specialists needed.

Movement Costs : these depend on the distance travelled and the route taken.

Transhipment costs : it adds to the cost to unload from one vehicle and load into another.

Unloading Costs : again involving labour.

Insurance Charges : these vary with the nature of the journey and the class of goods carried.

Costs of Documentation, Packaging and Storage at Depot : these must be added to those involved in the actual movement from X to Y.

Depreciation Costs : these relate to the capital assets of the whole transport system—e.g. railway depots, stations, track, etc.

To these is usually added a profit for the carrier.

This total is not necessarily the charge made to the consignee. Some routes may be subsidised at the expense of others, to encourage the use of one form of transport rather than another; or low rates may be offered to obtain a return load.

We need to appreciate the significance of these facts if we are to understand competition between various forms of transport and the reasons for the development of a pattern of communications.

Forms of Transport

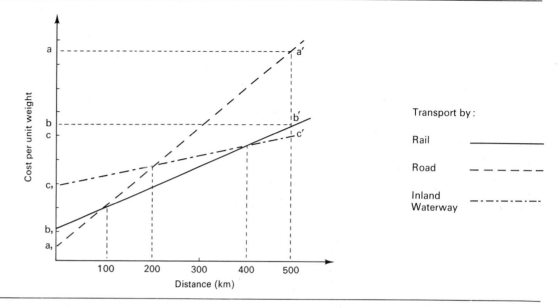

Fig. 106. Diagrammatic representation of the competitive advantages of road, rail, and waterways as freight carriers. The distances are purely illustrative, and the effects of tapering rates are not shown. The railway, of course, has the advantages in speed and bulk carried, and the road the advantages of flexibility and lower terminal costs.

Packaging and Bulk Carriage

In transporting goods in bulk, careful examination of the efficiency of the whole transport system may avoid heavy charges for break of bulk and tranship-ment. Various forms of pre-packed containers are now widely used. These can be transferred easily from, say, railway trucks to ships' hold, and thence to lorries at the delivery port: they may then travel to a single destination, or their own packaged con-tents may be redistributed as near to their various destinations as is economically feasible.

Each form of transport within the system has its own advantages and disadvantages, so that pas-sengers may need to use several types of vehicle in a single journey—e.g. taxi—rail transport—airport 'bus—plane—'bus—taxi. Consider, therefore, some of the relationships between various forms of trans-port and lines of communication.

Land Transport

By road: Cars and lorries are flexible in their move-ments and lead to a denser network of communi-cations than rail transport. The individual vehicles carry relatively small loads compared with a railway train; but the overheads of road hauliers are low compared with those of a railway company, though this depends on the number of vehicles involved.

Cost considerations are related to distance and the nature of the route, to the expense of overnight ac-commodation for drivers, and whether or not a return load is available. Road vehicles are, therefore, particularly suitable for fairly short hauls and for local collection/delivery work.

In large countries, like Australia, where a few large urban areas are widely spaced, the roads play a relatively small part in inter-city freight transport; but in Britain road transport handles more freight than rail does—both on a tonnage and ton-mileage basis. It is estimated, however, that at distances over

300–500 kilometres costs generally favour railways.
By rail: A railway train can move large numbers of people and a large volume of freight at a greater speed, and more safely, than road transport. Run-ning costs are low, especially for diesel locomotives; but fixed overhead costs are high, and much main-tenance is required for tracks, installations, etc.

The choice of route is obviously limited to existing lines, and may be further restricted by variations of gauge, as has happened in India and between State systems in Australia, where much conversion has been necessary.

In large countries like Australia and Canada, there are wide expanses of thinly populated land over which track must be maintained, but which provides little input of freight or passengers. These are lines of relatively infrequent traffic, though produce carried to and from remote ports—grain, timber, or minerals—is likely to be valuable freight, and there may be container traffic between closely settled areas at each end of a trans-continental link.

Trunk Routes

Fig. 107. The M1 Motorway and the main railway, between the East Midlands and London, run through rural country in south Bedfordshire; Harlington can be seen to the east. Each is a major artery for bulk transport and affects the local landscape relatively little, though the road feeding the M1 at Toddington (bottom left) has been widened and straightened. Just to the south the growing industrial town of Luton has benefited greatly from both trunk routes, and its overflow helps to feed the housing estates which can be seen spreading away from the old nucleus of Harlington, just east of the road-rail bridge.

The Port: A Nodal Point in a Transport System

The importance of considering transport systems as a whole has already been stressed. In the facing photographs we see arterial land-routes between inland industrial regions and one of the world's major city-ports, and the junction of the land and sea routes at one of the Docks. The sea is a major traffic medium; the volume of goods per unit carrier is great; it is expensive and creates bottlenecks if vessels are tied up for any length of time; and so the organisation of efficient land communications, with rapid delivery and removal by vehicles, is essential in order to keep the arteries clear for traffic movements, on which all trade is based. A careful study of this picture of Tilbury shows evidence of this organisation, and many of the activities described are seen in operation. Notice especially the two long container ships to the right, within the docks, one overshadowed by the gantry lifting its cargo; sixteen other vessels are berthed, one passing through the locks and one under tow.

Fig. 108. The main part of Tilbury Docks, seen from the north, with the Thames beyond. Australian, West African and Indian trades have been dominant features of the commerce of these docks. It has also long been a main passenger embarkation port for the Continent (its passenger stage is down-river of these docks). Now there are vehicle roll-on/roll-off Continental ferries, and developments which enable it to handle bulk goods in containers.

The convergence and overpasses of the land transport routes, seen in the photograph, the ordered rows of vehicles and stacked freight, the docked ships, and the barges stress the importance of such nodes in the transport systems. Tilbury has the advantage of being peripheral to the main built-up area of the metropolis; though this was a disadvantage when road traffic was slow, more than half the import tonnage is now carried by road; the Dartford-Purfleet tunnel carries goods south of the river.

Forms of Transport

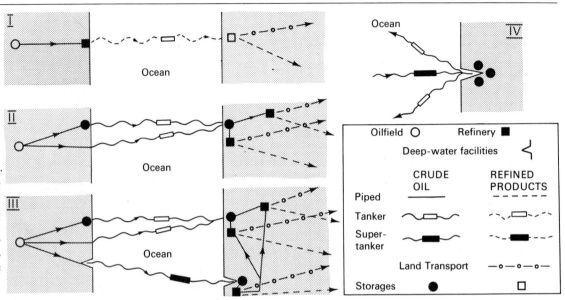

Fig. 109. *The changing roles of pipelines and ocean carriers in the oil industry.*

(I) represents a common situation up to early nineteen-fifties, when there was considerable sea transportation of refined products. (II) shows oil delivered by medium sized tankers to overseas storages, and the use of pipes for supplying refineries and distributing the products. (III) shows bulk carriers delivering to specially located deep-water terminals; pipelines feed refineries. (IV) shows bulk storage depots near very deep anchorages, served by huge carriers, and re-distribution by smaller tankers. Mammoth tankers can, in fact, already supply smaller tankers direct.

Traffic-flow on the railways is apt to be uneven. Commuter traffic may be heavy for only five days a week, and even then concentrated mainly in the early morning and early evening; there is also heavy holiday traffic to resorts, or to ports, at certain times of the year. This is likely to lead to a costly service.

In countries like Britain, whose rail networks were well established before the motor vehicle arrived, and at a time when railway company rivalry led to a proliferation of tracks, many lines have come to carry only a tiny proportion of the traffic of the whole system, and have become uneconomic to maintain.

Overall, therefore, rail transport is relatively inflexible and can achieve greatest economies when a full freight load is carried over long distances, and when freight handlings can be mechanised, as with container carriage by freight-liner trains.

Pipelines: These are, of course, inflexible and cost a great deal to install. They are vulnerable not only to physical disruption, but also to shifts in fortune of the producing sources and of the markets. How-ever, they have long been used for carrying water—of low value and used in very large quantities.

Gas and oil pipelines have been in use for more than a century, and pipe networks carry manufactured and natural gas, crude oil, and refined products.

A much wider use is now made of pipelines. They have begun to be used to carry, for instance, coal (as a crushed slurry, with water), finely crushed limestone, chemical materials, and even milk.

As part of a general transport system, linked to transport by ocean vessels and land tankers, they are best seen in use in the world-wide oil and petrochemical industries (Fig. 109).

Water Transport

Ocean Vessels: The cost of freight movement by ship is relatively low, especially by large vessels, which on a capacity-cost basis are cheaper to build, run, and maintain than smaller vessels making up an equivalent tonnage. As a result the size of cargo vessels has greatly increased in recent years.

This has affected the routes used. Linking waterways, such as the Panama and Suez canals, when operational, are focal points for many lines; but obviously there are limits to the size of vessel able to pass through. The tendency is also for very large ships to dock at relatively few deep-water terminals. Certain entrepôt ports, like London and Rotterdam, have long received bulk cargoes, which are broken down for re-distribution by smaller carriers. The introduction of very large bulk carriers has emphasised the importance of deep-water terminals, which can either receive a particular commodity for storage and re-distribution—oil or ores, for example—or can quickly turn round bulk-container carriers, and quickly despatch containers by land transport.

This has meant developing new terminals, as in deep-water Bantry Bay in south-western Ireland, and at Europort-Rotterdam, artificially deepened to receive oil and ore vessels.

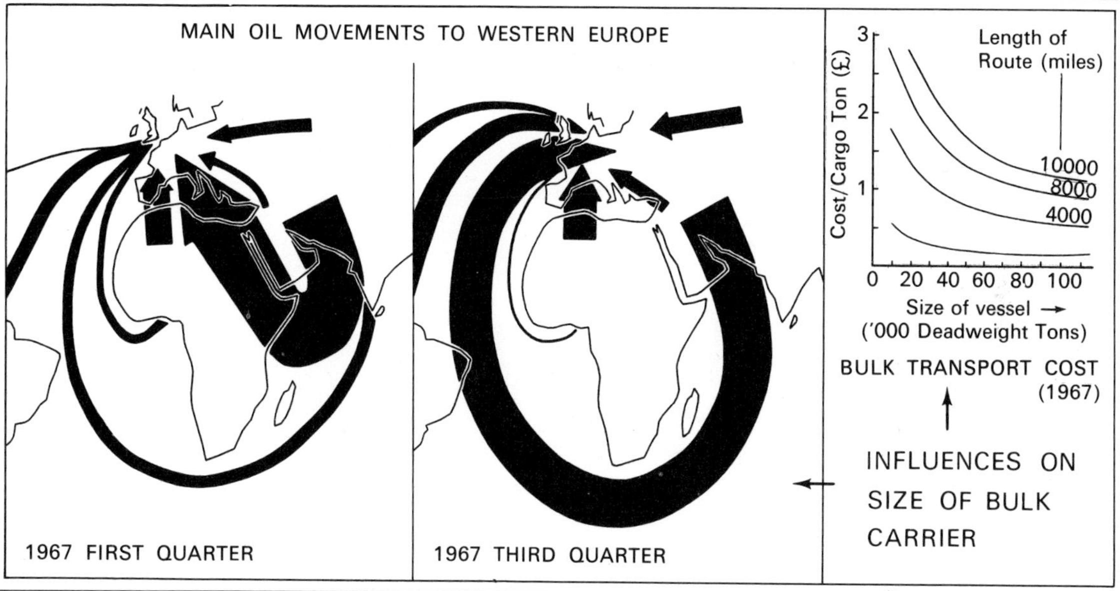

Influences on Freight Movements

MAIN OIL MOVEMENTS TO WESTERN EUROPE

1967 FIRST QUARTER

1967 THIRD QUARTER

BULK TRANSPORT COST (1967)

← INFLUENCES ON SIZE OF BULK CARRIER

Cost/Cargo Ton (£)

Length of Route (miles)
10000
8000
4000

Size of vessel → ('000 Deadweight Tons)

Fig. 110. Hostile actions and political barriers seem, unfortunately, to be universal adjuncts to man's settlements. Their effects are often far reaching. Here the economic facts of long-distance transport are viewed in the light of the re-routing of oil supplies caused by events in the Middle East and Nigeria. The enormous increase in cargo-ton-mileage makes it desirable to use a fleet of very large bulk carriers.

Terminal charges at a port are high and, as a vessel is not earning while tied up, a quick turn-round is essential. The relative slowness of travel of the individual vessel does not matter quite so much, provided another is following to be unloaded in its turn, as part of a 'chain of delivery'—though, again, wages, insurance and maintenance of a number of smaller, slower vessels is more costly than if fewer, speedier, vessels of equivalent cargo capacity are operating.

Ships should be loaded to capacity and ensured of a return cargo if possible. Some vessels carry both liquid and dry cargoes in separate holds, some have convertible holds for different types of cargo. Those with a one-way delivery run, oil- and ore-tankers for instance, are often leased by companies on long-term charters with special financial arrangements, in order to cut costs. With shipping, therefore, there is close connection between costing and routes.

Inland Waterways: The use of a navigable river as part of a major transport system depends greatly on its alignment relative to large centres of population,

resources, industries, and existing trade-routes. While the Rhine is an immensely important commercial artery, serving many major industrial regions between Basle and Europort, the Amazon river system, with deep water extending into the heart of a land-mass carries few commercial vessels.

Canals and canalised waterways are used where water transport is economically desirable and natural waterways unsuitable. There are usually very high initial costs of construction. In northern Britain, many tunnels and locks were constructed to create the, now obsolete, canal network which helped the large-scale manufacturing and commercial developments of the nineteenth century. Recently, on a different scale, there has been great investment in the St. Lawrence Seaway, which links the lakeside ports of Canada and the USA with the Atlantic. Despite the drawback of the winter freeze, the waterway has aided industrial production, especially near Montreal, where hydroelectric energy is available.

Locks slow up transport, though some countries

with low relief, like the Netherlands, can develop wide waterways with a minimum of locks, and use relatively fast-moving vessels. In this latter case, the canal networks and links are very much a part of the whole transport system of north-west Europe.

On inland waterways the cargoes are mostly non-perishable and can be stored, so that the speed of a vessel need not be a vital factor.

Air Transport

The development of new aircraft involves great expense and much time, and it is difficult to foresee the nature of future competition.

Aircraft capacity is small, and though high speeds and a quick turn-round are compensating factors, the fuel consumption is high, particularly on take-off. This makes short-hauls economically unattractive. As terminal charges are high, this form of transport is generally most suitable for high-priced goods and passengers carried over long distances.

The Integration of Land and Water Transport Systems

Fig. 111. Across the St. Lawrence river the wooded heights of Mount Royal rise up behind Montreal's Central Business District. Above the docks (D)—Fig. 112—the river is unnavigable for large shipping; ships enter the docks through a dredged channel.

This great city and industrial port is a major route-focus and place of interchange for rail, road, river, canal, and air transport. Here a ship passes from the St. Lawrence Seaway through the St. Lambert Lock (L), prior to entering the main river. The split rail system (R) enables trains to continue across one arm when the other is broken as the track is raised to enable a ship to enter or leave the lock.

Fig. 112. River, Seaway, Road and Rail at Montreal.

D Dredged
Flow
Shallow River
R
Seaway
L
0 km 1
Road —
Railway +——+

Fig. 113. (above) A container from the aluminium works at Bell Bay, on the Tamar river estuary in northern Tasmania, is being lifted from a lorry for transhipment.

There are two types of bulk-handling facilities here. One, like this, for the despatch of special forms of processed metal; the other for unloading and delivering alumina and ores for ferro-manganese products, brought by ships for the nearby industrial plants, which make use of Tasmania's abundant and cheap power supplies.

Apart from the establishment of routes of communication, close integration of the various forms of transport within a system is needed to ensure that time is not lost, either en route (Fig. 111) or at places of transfer—docksides, stations, airports, depots.

Containers make for efficiency and rapid transfer of bulk loads from one form of transport to another, and are easily stacked for carriage. The moving belts for the ores at Bell Bay and the suction pipes at Montreal's grain storages and flour mills, near the docks, are other practical means of speeding 'turn-round'.

Air Transport

Route Densities

Fig. 114. Economic development and route densities are closely related. I shows significant density differences of main roads in 4 km² about the centre of two towns on Midland clay vales—Bedford with developing industries (pp. 120–125) and Thame, which retains its market functions, but is virtually non-industrial.

The connectivity of rail networks has also been found to correlate strongly with the stages of economic development of countries. The so-called β-Index[6] is one expression of connectivity, and is found by dividing the number of vertices (i.e. towns, or road-intersections) into the number of edges ('edge' ≡ railway, or road, joining two vertices). II has only one circuit (β=1); III has only partial connections; in IV they are more complex (β=1·25).

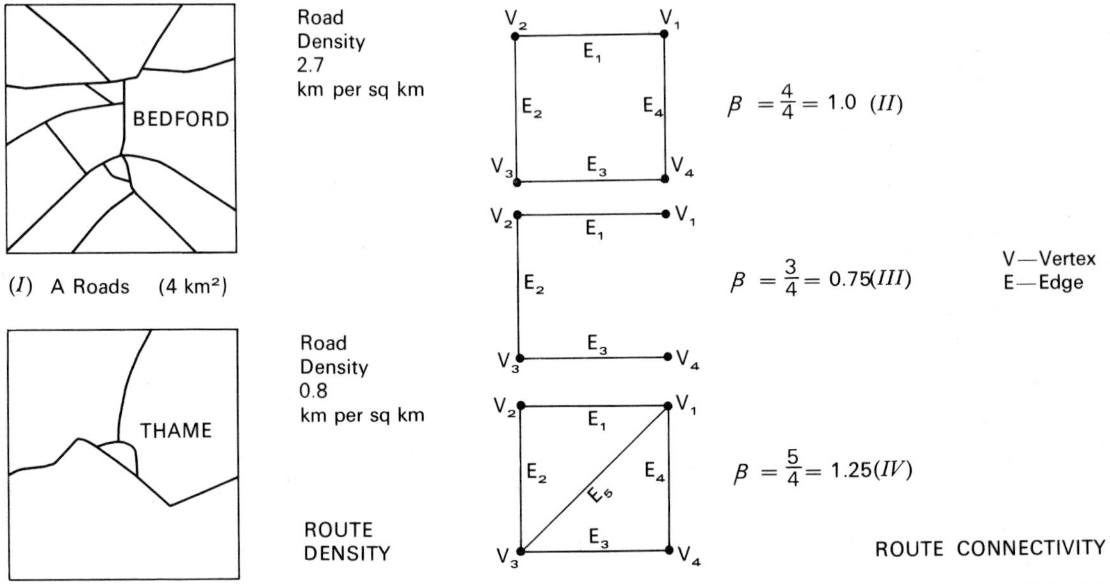

$$\beta = \frac{4}{4} = 1.0 \ (II)$$

$$\beta = \frac{3}{4} = 0.75 \ (III)$$

$$\beta = \frac{5}{4} = 1.25 \ (IV)$$

V—Vertex
E—Edge

ROUTE CONNECTIVITY

The terminal facilities at large airports occupy a huge area, and the runways are long, so that, for safety's sake also, airports are relatively far from the cities they serve. The routes and mode of transport from city terminals to airports are important factors in transport systems, and time between them a vital consideration in planning.

Aircraft routes are apparently unlimited, but in fact controlled by a number of important factors. Apart from flight channels which must be rigidly adhered to for safety, the routes taken by aircraft depend on political barriers, the precise location of the terminal airports, the need for refuelling, and the necessity of picking up the maximum number of passengers or greatest load of freight. Thus a charter flight from England to Australia, with a full complement guaranteed, may stop to refuel at Tehran and Singapore; while aircraft on a scheduled service between the two may stop at Athens, Tehran, New Delhi, and Bangkok, and continue to Hong Kong and Manilla before flying on to Sydney. At each airport different passengers may board or leave.

Some aircraft perform special roles, especially for remote settlements. Over the Canadian Shield, small aircraft with floats or skis serves scattered settlements throughout the year. In Australia, the Royal Flying Doctor Service helps communities in remote places under difficult conditions. Specially constructed aircraft can move heavy equipment far beyond existing road or rail.

Aircraft should be seen as part of a whole transport system, for at their destination there is usually a transfer to another form of transport.

Patterns of Communication

Route Density and Economic Development

The density of transport routes (networks) is usually closely connected with the general economic development of the area concerned; though, of course,

'route' should be carefully defined—whether, for instance, a track, or a road capable of carrying normal self-propelled vehicles.

A ranking of national road densities shows that the first eleven countries are in Western Europe, beginning with the UK, Western Germany, Belgium, and France. European countries also lead in the ranking of railway density patterns.

Most of the underdeveloped countries are at the other end of the scale, especially in railway ranking; though some, like India, whose railway systems were developed mostly under British administration, rank relatively high.

If we further consider correlations between densities and 'developed' or 'under-developed' countries, we find other apparent anomalies. For instance, 'developed' countries with large land areas where population and industries are concentrated in certain parts of the country, as in Canada, rank lower than one might expect if 'development' alone were the criterion.

Route Connections and Patterns

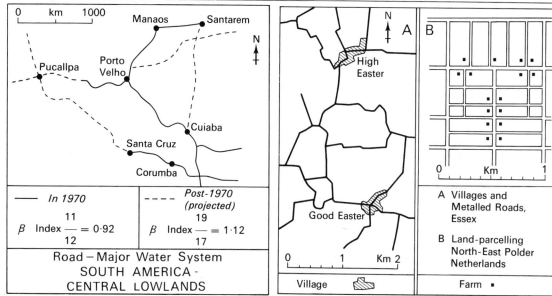

Fig. 115. Changes in connectivity and increasing integration within the Amazon-Parana lowlands as projected routeways are completed. Comparisons are made in terms of the β-Index.

Fig. 116. In the lowlands of rural Essex, patterns of settlement have slowly evolved, and country roads and tracks deviate about old field boundaries. The Easters take their name from the Anglo-Saxon for sheep-fold, and the earliest maps show devious paths between them. In contrast, the ordered settlement pattern of the Netherlands polders reflects carefully planned use of a flat, uniform landscape.

We should also be aware of the dangers of attempting to draw conclusions from a comparison of route densities alone. Some railways and roads have multiple tracks or lanes, though, of course, schemes may be devised to allow for this.

Below national level, much depends on the nature of the region considered. It is not always easy, even with careful correlation techniques, to find explanations for particular densities. Obviously a favourable physical environment (a fertile plain, say) or an unfavourable one (a swamp or salt-lake) is likely to affect route density directly and commercial activities in a well-developed part of the region will probably lead to a close route network; but the actual density may depend a great deal on the situation of the whole region. A location *between* other areas of close population may well result in a density of traffic lanes within the region greater than one would otherwise expect, as we find in the Albany-Schenectady region of the upper Hudson valley in New York State.

In any settlement study, rural or urban, it is an instructive preliminary to observe the differences in route density shown by a large-scale map: close nets about towns and villages, compared with open networks in the surrounding countryside; dense street patterns in nineteenth-century industrial parts of large cities in Britain, compared with more open geometric, curved patterns of recent suburban development or new industrial estates, see Fig. 148.

Quantitative studies may be made by measuring the length of road per unit area; or, closely correlated with this, the density of road junctions, particularly in urban districts. The zones of network density may then be plotted. The result may indicate regular patterns related to old or new commercial districts, suburban development centres, and so on.

Route Patterns: Their Evolution

Figs. 116 and 120 show some of the route patterns developed under different circumstances: devious routes about rural centres in an old-established

landscape; a rectangular pattern in more recently developed country; and systems branching from those ports of entry vital to early development.

In the first case (Fig. 116 A) the routes between one settlement and the next follow more or less complex paths, rather than straight lines. Positive and negative deviations (p. 25) occur in response to physical obstacles, existing land-holdings, and other historic influences. The route pattern of the whole of this part of Essex is complex, yet the overall appearance is that expected of rural central places, spaced more or less equidistant from others of the same order, and each the focus of a number of routes.

Fig. 116 B is Dutch polder settlement, typical of the geometric forms often adopted for planned settlement in open country. This is seen in the old Roman centuriated pattern in the Pontine Marshes, and in the 'new' North American Mid-West and Prairies, where the original square townships, nested sections of one mile square, and quarter-sections (160 acres), survive in present settlement patterns.

Transport and Commercial Activities

Fig. 117. Fishing vessels unloading at North Shields, on Tyneside. The role of land transport in the fishing industry is emphasised by the railway sidings along the wharves, the waiting lorries, and the piles of ice and salt—all needed to transport fresh fish rapidly to urban markets.

Routeways, Transport and Central Places

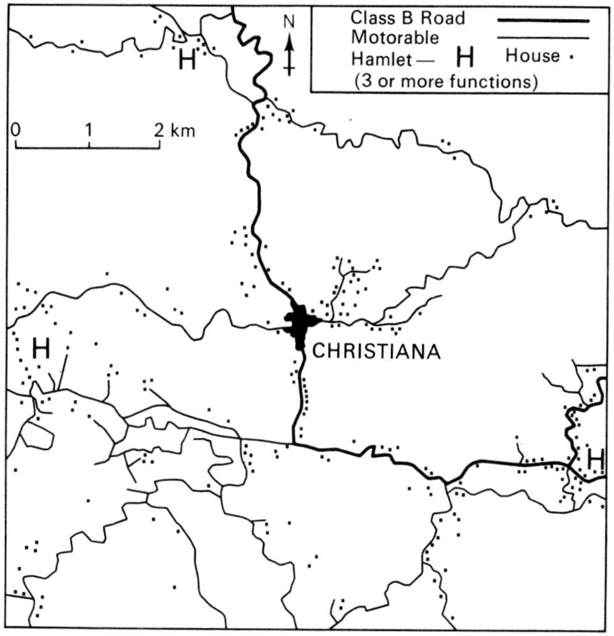

Fig. 118. Christiana is located among broken, hilly country in central Jamaica—notice the bends on the roads. The farming population, although dispersed in small units, remains fairly close to the roads, especially in the valleys, where small clusters, hamlets, develop. In general, Christiana provides the majority of the central place functions for a wide area—churches, the larger schools, shops, garage, hotels, betting offices, and facilities for open marketing. It receives and distributes goods from Kingston, and collects and despatches produce from the countryside. The metalled, Class B, road is the main artery enabling Christiana to act as an efficient regional market town; the network of smaller, motorable roads ensure its vitality, obvious in the scene in Fig. 119.

Fig. 119. Christiana, in central Jamaica; a busy market town. People from outlying districts come in by bus, cars, animal transport and on foot. The shops are well stocked, but market transactions also take place in the open.

91

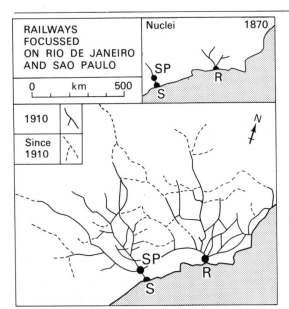

RAILWAYS
FOCUSSED
ON RIO DE JANEIRO
AND SAO PAULO

0   km   500

Nuclei   1870
SP
R
S

1910

Since
1910

N

SP
S
R

Route Patterns and Accessibility

Fig. 120. By 1910 railway construction spreading from Rio de Janeiro (R) and Santos-São Paulo (S-SP) had created arterial systems, linked only by the direct, southern, inter-city line. The routes focused on the expanding cities, though lateral lines were already linking some inland centres.

Subsequent developments have led to the closer integration of the two separate systems.

Fig. 121. Before the opening of the Severn Bridge (Br) in the 'sixties, the lowest bridging point for road traffic was Gloucester (G). The map shows increased accessibility, re-lated to Monmouth (M), Newport (N), Bristol (B), and Weston-super-Mare (W).

Remember, however, that accessibility should also be con-sidered on a journey-time basis, in which road conditions and traffic flow are also limiting factors.

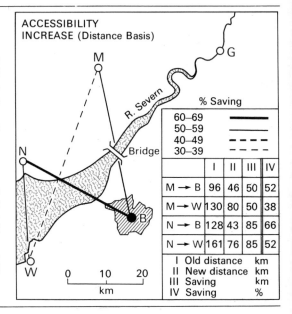

ACCESSIBILITY
INCREASE (Distance Basis)

M   G
R. Severn
N   Bridge

% Saving

60–69	
50–59	
40–49	
30–39	

B

W

0   10   20
km

	I	II	III	IV
M → B	96	46	50	52
M → W	130	80	50	38
N → B	128	43	85	66
N → W	161	76	85	52

I Old distance	km
II New distance	km
III Saving	km
IV Saving	%

In Fig. 120, route patterns have evolved in stages. At first pioneer routes led from ports into the interior, becoming the established links with developing inland trading centres. As a port's hinterland grew, routes from various parts came to focus on the expanding port. Other interior routes then began to feed into these now main arteries of communication, which became linked by lateral routes. As intermediate settlement developed and some inland centres became particularly important, the routes running from these to the port became major ones.

Changes in Existing Route Patterns

A developed network may become 'dated' as new forms of transport are introduced and new places of prominence arise within it. It may become desirable to create a straightforward connecting link between two prominent places, irrespective of intervening centres of settlement, which may be by-passed. The 'through' transport route so created will

almost certainly affect the accessibility, and may alter the functions, of towns close to it, and so, in time, affect the overall pattern of routeways.

Settlements located near major junctions with the through-road may gain advantages; but it would seem that others, being by-passed, would decline. This is not necessarily so. An inherited disadvantage of early road systems is that main roads almost always pass through the middle of a town. Heavy through-traffic may, therefore, have so paralysed a market town, bringing traffic jams, parking problems, and overcrowding, that, as a central commercial place, it may have already have become unattractive to shoppers from surrounding areas and to regional businessmen. A by-pass may, therefore, relieve these conditions, and once more stimulate local trade and services. Being a pleasanter place to live in, the town may then find itself developing as a residential settlement, and so changing its character—in many ways for the better.

Creating a link between transport networks can

have instant effects; in the way that the completion of the Severn Bridge allowed motorway links between Bristol and South Wales, which not only saved distance and the road congestion on the old route via Gloucester, but brought close, in distance and time, the considerable concentrations of population about Bristol and Severnside and those of industrial South Wales. Other effects were the increased accessibility of the Forest of Dean and the Welsh valleys to the people of south-west England. Movements in the other direction included the greatly increased short-time tourist visits to Weston-super-Mare and other parts of Somerset, and Bristol became the major commercial service centre for many people west of the Severn.

Interconnection is thus a very real factor in the efficiency of transport systems, and affects the activities of large numbers of people. For this reason, there is real value in studying the efficiency of transport networks in terms of the various uses made of them by people living in, or moving through, the area.

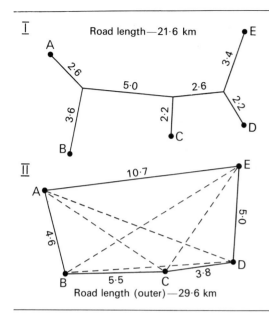

I — Road length—21.6 km

II — Road length (outer)—29.6 km

Route Links and Networks

Fig. 122. I shows a set of road links between villages A, B, C, D, E ; not necessarily the shortest set which could exist. (β-Index = 1·14).
II shows a road added to allow a continuous journey around all five villages (β = 1·00), and also, by broken lines, roads which complete a fully linked network (β = 1·50).

Fig. 123. A network showing the order of sealed roads within Western Australia, with Perth as the pole (outlet). The circuit is simplified by breaks in the closed loops of the roads (creating a 'watershed' in each case from which traffic flows to one or other of the main roads (channels)).

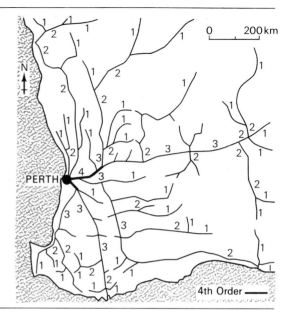

Creating Efficient Networks

When trying to create an efficient route system, it is, of course, important to keep in mind who is to benefit from the ultimate arrangement. It should then be possible to devise a theoretical system to be of maximum benefit to that group of persons.

If settlements A, B, C, D, E are to be so linked that the minimum is spent on road building to a specified standard, then one would recommend a system such as that in Fig. 122 (I) (though determining first the *shortest set* of lines[7]).

Suppose, however, you are concerned that the traveller who must regularly visit each place in turn does not waste time retracing his steps, then a system like that in Fig. 122 (II) would shorten the round trip to include each settlement. In this case, greater length of routeway must be constructed, at greater cost. The journeys between individual places are not necessarily shorter: here A to E is much shorter, but A to D is longer.

It is possible to build a network which would link any place with all the others by the most direct path, as shown by the broken lines in Fig. 122 (II). The costs of construction and maintenance would be great, but the user would benefit by taking the shorter journey to any centre.

In terms of railway construction, the latter solution is likely to be favourable in a closely settled area with large population centres and much traffic between them. The return from fares would be great, and the lay-out would serve the user well.

In a sparsely settled area, where the lines are likely to be used less often, a pattern which would limit construction costs is more practical.

If many points (settlements) are involved, possible solutions may run into millions, and high-speed computers are needed to give the most feasible arrangements. Minimisation solutions are sought for other problems, such as possible arrangements of farms or factories in relation to service roads to enable them to function efficiently.

Studying Existing Routes

Distinct close networks of routes may be seen in economically important parts of a country. These may be linked by trunk routes which tap the feeder systems of each of the well-developed areas.

If a major reference point is considered (the capital city, or main port, perhaps) with its own route system, this may be seen to resemble a 'drainage system', with sets of routes arranged in branching, tributary fashion, with the major reference point its outlet (as to the sea).

It is possible to assign orders of importance to routes, similar to 'stream orders'. In countries with large, complex route circuits, it is only possible to do this if each individual circuit is simplified. Ways of doing this have been postulated; but here we may simply take note of it as an example of how modern geographers seek to transform complexities into simple forms, which may then be studied in relation to the physical and human environment.

Rectangular Patterns on Extensive Plains

Fig. 124. A rectangular settlement pattern in mid-Iowa, characteristic of the American plainlands, with farms on their blocks of land, sheltered by trees; the rectangular strip-cultivation helps to check erosion.

The individual farms are the smallest units in a hierarchy of places, which in Iowa ascend from the small 'convenience-goods centres' of a few hundred folk, through 'shopping-goods centres', 'speciality-goods centres', and 'wholesale-goods' towns and cities, with size sequences of the order of 1500; 6000; 60 000; 250 000, and over a million—maintained at appropriately spaced intervals by the regularity of road systems, as seen here.

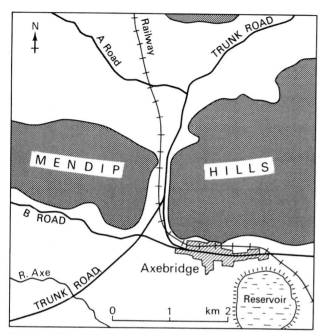

Fig. 125. Key to Fig. 126, showing the route concentration and the location of Axebridge.

Fig. 126. Gap through the Mendip Hills west of Axebridge, which can be seen to the right on the lower slopes, above the flood-plain of the river Axe. The main routes from western and central Somerset pass through the Mendips, northwards to Bristol, without a steep hill-climb like those at Wells, to the east of this.

We have seen that the patterns of settlements and their inter-communications depend to a large extent on economic considerations—the clustering of retail and service businesses in market centres which serve surrounding populations, in competition with other centres.

But, though relief alone does not usually account for an overall settlement pattern, we must remember that physical features have considerable influence on the forms of land-use, local siting of settlements, and alignment of communications—witness the land-use on the Mendips and in the vales, the site of Axebridge, and the patterns of roads and railway seen in Fig. 126.

95

Chapter VII
Urban Location, Size and Spacing

Settlement Size and Functions

Fig. 127. In (I) we see that various functions (such as a branch bank, petrol station, grocery store, or hairdresser) each need a certain number of customers to support them—the threshold number.

(II) shows that in the area under consideration only one unit of type A is possible (because of the restricted number of potential users); but there could be twenty units of type D in the various settlements within this area. (This is a highly theoretical approach of course, and takes no account, for instance, of consumers passing through the area.)

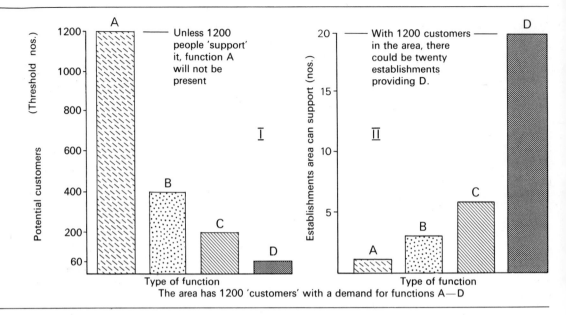

I — Unless 1200 people 'support' it, function A will not be present

II — With 1200 customers in the area, there could be twenty establishments providing D.

(Threshold nos.) / Potential customers / Type of function

Establishments area can support (nos.) / Type of function

The area has 1200 'customers' with a demand for functions A—D

Urban Settlement—Types and Distribution

We have already seen something of the growth of urban clusters and of large commercial, industrial, and multifunctional cities (Chap. IV). Here we look rather more closely at the patterns of urban development, and the relationships between towns and other settlements of a lower and higher order—for in many, though certainly not all, areas of settlement there is a measure of order in the ranking and spatial distribution of population clusters.

Urban settlements are multifunctional, and indeed the presence of various functions and the number of functional units in a town may be used as guides to its ranking in any hierarchy of settlements. Towns are sometimes termed 'Commercial', 'Industrial', 'Administrative', or whatever, in terms of their functions; but this is bound to be an imprecise description. Yet there is logic in distinguishing urban groups with related functions, provided we realise

that there is bound to be overlapping, and that from time to time functions are acquired or shed.

Among such distinct groups are commercial 'central place' settlements, primarily serving and drawing custom from surrounding areas. There are also urban centres with well-developed specialist industries, serving not only a local population but also a much wider area, perhaps international; these are typified by the older coalfield manufacturing towns in Britain, and also by the strips of modern resort towns along the coasts.

In any broad area of modern occupation, with such a variety of urban places among the hamlets and villages of earlier development, it would appear unlikely that one would find ordered groups of settlements. Yet there are often observable regularities in spacing between villages, towns and cities which seem to relate to the various theories of regular central place 'hierarchies'. Then there seems to be strong evidence of relationships between functions (and numbers of functional units) and the size, and

especially status, of settlements—hamlets, villages, towns. There is also evidence of a regular progression of population size from largest city to the smallest settlement, and of significant breaks in this progression (p. 100), which some relate to Christaller's hierarchies, though this is debatable.

Population Clusters and Central Places

Activities necessary for the welfare of any community are usually most efficiently carried out if the people involved are clustered together. They may, of course, serve the needs of surrounding tributary areas as well as their own. Such a 'central place' is a focus at which groups of activities are concentrated—separated from other nodal clusters but linked to them by transport routes. Each is a node in a transport network; a commercial place, usually with strong market functions.

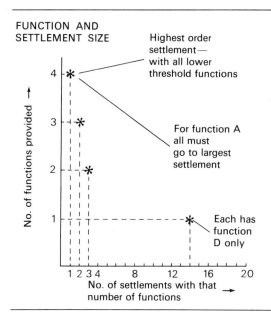

FUNCTION AND SETTLEMENT SIZE

Highest order settlement— with all lower threshold functions

For function A all must go to largest settlement

Each has function D only

No. of functions provided ↑

No. of settlements with that number of functions →

Goods and Services Offered

Fig. 128. In this case the highest order settlement in the area provides one of each of the four functions. People must travel here if they wish to make use of function A. Assuming that there is no more than one unit of each function (not always the case in reality), we may now work out the number of settlements able to supply three, two, or simply one function, as shown on the graph.

Fig. 129. Order now appears among the settlements. One serves at least 1200 people (for function A); two serve not less than 400, with B, C, and D; three supply C and D; and fourteen each provide D for at least 60 people. The figure shows diagrammatically, how a plot of the area served against the numbers served may show an ordered distribution of settlements. In fact, with many people clustered near a first order settlement it is likely that it will contain more than one functional unit of C and D—see Fig. 143.

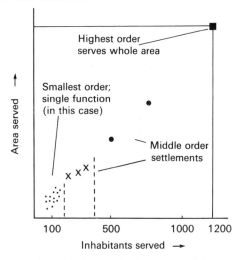

ORDER, SIZE AND SERVICE OF SETTLEMENTS

Highest order serves whole area

Smallest order; single function (in this case)

Middle order settlements

Area served ↑

Inhabitants served →

Market Functions—Threshold and Range

The concept of a 'market threshold' is important here. This means that a good or service will not be offered at a particular central place unless there is sufficient demand for it in the area served. If the market area increases, or for some reason the people acquire a greater purchasing power, demand may become sufficiently great to make it profitable for that place to offer that good or service—for which a necessary 'threshold' will have been reached.

Linked with this is the concept of distance, or 'range', through which people are prepared to travel to the central place to purchase a good, or make use of a service. Some commodities in daily use, such as bread and household 'convenience goods', would generally be offered fairly locally; 'durable goods' in periodic demand, such as furniture or jewellery, may only be available in a higher order settlement, in which outsiders would shop occasionally.

Looking at this another way; a particular settlement in the hierarchy 'hamlet, village, town, city' would offer goods or services appropriate to its class or order. A lower order place (a small village) would offer only a limited number of goods or services for its own population and for that of the immediate surroundings; it may have a church, primary school, general store, post office and filling station. A place of the next higher order (a small town), serving a larger population and wider area, may include in its services a bank, small hospital, secondary school, department store, hairdressers, service garage, etc.

Functions, Order, and Size of Settlements

Some functions are acquired as a commercial threshold is reached. Others are attracted by an available source of labour as well as by the opportunity of catering for the need of a large local population. They may then, in their turn, offer extra

employment; a new factory may attract other workers from outside. Hence the increases of both population and functions are closely inter-connected. This tends to result in a 'jump' in population size from one order of settlement, offering a limited range of goods and services, to a higher order settlement, which offers more and employs more people.

The same naturally applies to commercial functions. Certain numbers are employed in a central place to supply goods to lower order settlements about it; the latter supply fewer goods to their local countryside and employ fewer people in their distribution. The movement is often two-way; with goods going from farms to urban markets, and goods and services from city to town, to village, to rural consumer. But, as will become apparent, there is not necessarily a regular transfer of goods from step to step through the hierarchy. Goods may be despatched direct from farm to urban collecting centre, while a farm, or village store, may receive goods direct from the city.

Rural Centre with Few Functions

Fig. 130. Castle Camps, amid arable, pasture, and orchards. The large, once-moated, farm (right) employs local men in specialised pig, cattle, and animal feed production. The village is of the country and serves its local population; before the Black Death, its centre was a kilometre south, next to the double moat enclosing castle and church.

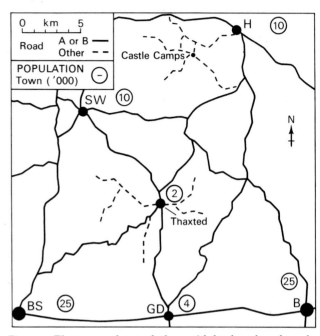

Fig. 131. The two rural central places with local roads and nearby towns. Minor roads are shown only in the immediate vicinity of Thaxted and Castle Camps.

The two communities can be compared in terms of size and functions. Thaxted, with about 2000 people, has some five dozen functional units, other than residencies, compared with a dozen at Castle Camps (pop. 200); these include the great church, several chapels, some thirty retail establishments (including six antique shops), inns, pubs, restaurants and cafés, branch stores and branch bank, main post office, estate agents, bookshops, hairdressers, and garages.

Castle Camps serves a very local rural population; its dozen units include a small school, chapel, inn, two pubs, and three general stores (one a post office).

Rural Centre: More Functions, More Functional Units

Fig. 132. Thaxted, in rural Essex, has always been a central market place with special functions. In the 14th century the craftsmanship of its cutlery brought prosperity; the great church and guildhall of that period still dominate the wide market street of the town's chief axis. When cutlery declined, cloth-making became a dominant industry. Now, with the beauty of its setting and old buildings, tourism flourishes. Yet it remains what it has always been—a central place serving a fertile agricultural area.

Ordered Arrangements of Settlements

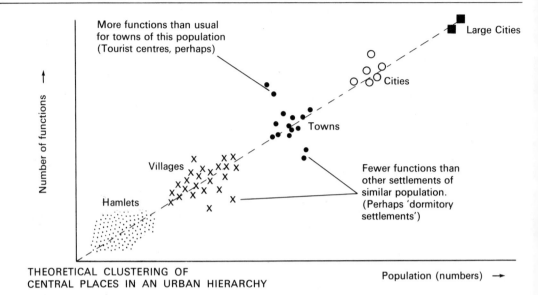

More functions than usual
for towns of this population
(Tourist centres, perhaps)

Large Cities

Cities

Towns

Villages

Hamlets

Fewer functions than
other settlements of
similar population.
(Perhaps 'dormitory
settlements')

Number of functions

THEORETICAL CLUSTERING OF
CENTRAL PLACES IN AN URBAN HIERARCHY

Population (numbers) →

Fig. 133. The hierarchy of central places, from hamlets with few functions to cities with many, is expressed here in an idealised plot. There will, of course, be anomalies, for not all towns function as 'central places'. This would be so with a tourist town, which usually has more functions than the size of its resident population would indicate. On the other hand, dormitory settlements, which are bases for commuting, tend to have fewer functions than service towns of similar population.

By plotting the population of central places against their functions we may look for distinct clusters of places on the graph, with those small centres, with few different functions, separated by a population 'jump' from larger ones with many different functions, and may differentiate first-order 'hamlets' from second-order 'villages' and so on (Fig. 133).

Places of a higher order not only include functions which are not present in lower order places, but they usually have more shops, garages, etc. (more 'functional units'). If the number of different functions are plotted against the total number of functional units for each settlement in a given area, we may again look for groupings in orders, related to the hierarchy from hamlet to city (Fig. 143).

Commercial Central Places and Their Ordered Arrangement

We may now look for regularities in the distances between settlements of the same size-class. There

will be commercial competition between places of a similar order; and, if the system of transportation is well developed, the consequent sharing of custom between markets should result in a more or less regular pattern of commercial central places. But, as Christaller postulated, this will depend on a uniform distribution of population, purchasing power and resources, uniform physical conditions, and equal transport facilities in all directions.

As we study the lattice models of settlement and trade area boundaries, we may again reflect that such conditions are unlikely to prevail. The central places are not usually the sole providers of services in an area; in practice the 'spheres of influence' of neighbouring centres overlap; also the presence of a large urban centre tends to discourage the growth of smaller adjacent centres at the distance suggested by the model; a large city may provide services which it would be uneconomic to duplicate in smaller centres, whose functions and size may thus be restricted.

These, and other objections may be valid. Never-

theless, such central-place models have greatly influenced modern geographical thinking. We may profitably consider why there are discrepancies between such theoretical arrangements and those we see on the ground.

Christaller's Central Place Models

Christaller noted, in southern Germany, the tendency for commercial central places, with their hexagonal hinterlands, to order themselves in a ratio of three; he put forward a model with the arrangement known as a k=3 hierarchy (Fig. 134).

This shows places with common levels of specialisation equally spaced. Hamlets are three times as numerous as villages, which are three times as numerous as towns. The town's hinterland is three times that of the village, and it has three times the population, and three times the purchasing power.

Fig. 134 shows the custom drawn from the next lower order settlements served by each central place (in terms of units of settlement). This is, of course

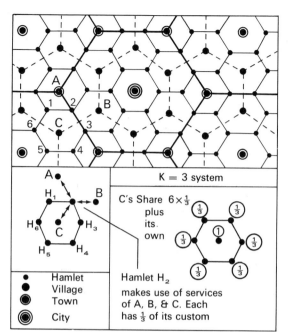

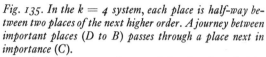

Hierarchy of Central Places—Models

Fig. 134. The k = 3 system depends on a marketing principle. Here we see a central place sharing the custom of a next lower order place with two settlements of its own size. Six equidistant lower order places provide six one-third shares of custom, to add to its own local custom.

Fig. 135. In the k = 4 system, each place is half-way between two places of the next higher order. A journey between important places (D to B) passes through a place next in importance (C).

In the k = 7 system, the central place has firm administrative control over the six dependent places, as indicated by the arrows.

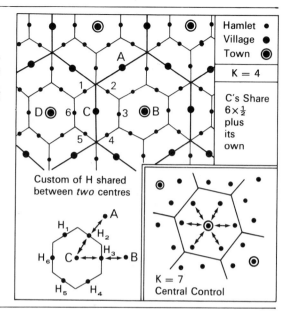

the *k* value—three in this case. There are six villages about each town, but each village shares its custom between three towns from which it is equidistant. Thus each town has six one-third 'allegiances' (i.e.—two) to add to its own, giving it a custom of three.

The actual spacing between settlements depends on the population density in the area at the time the settlement pattern evolved, and also of transport facilities. The market-hamlets (small villages) in southern Germany developed, in the days of animal transport, at an average distance of 7 km from one another, and the small townships 12 km apart ($\sqrt{3} \times 7$ km on the k=3 model).

The hexagonal spatial arrangement continues up to the largest city, whose hinterland is the whole area concerned, and for which it provides very special services and goods together with overall administration, being the central regional city.

This whole k=3 network is governed by marketing and supply considerations, however a k=4 system may be more a realistic portrayal of present arrange-

ments. In this system, as many important places as possible lie on one traffic route—an important consideration where cost of route construction is concerned. Here, as Fig. 135 shows, the border settlements share their custom between only two central places. Each central place therefore has six half-allegiances (i.e. three) to add to its own, a custom of four in all.

In circumstances where firm administrative control from a single central place is important, a k=7 system may be established, with six small settlements each controlled by a larger one, which has the custom of all six, plus its own; seven in all.

Other theoretical models have more sophisticated systems, some with variable *k* values; but the examples shown indicate order in the landscape, especially under conditions approaching those postulated by Christaller. They also enable us to consider the reasons for departures from the expected distribution of settlements.

Some towns, of course, have never been part of

the rigid hierarchy of central places; they may perhaps be 'historic relics', though some may have acquired the functions of service centres later; and we have already taken note of modern manufacturing towns whose main functions are concerned with consumers far beyond their own locality. When we construct plots relating size and function, such towns tend to be separated graphically from the distinct size-classes which indicate regular orders of settlements. We may also illustrate this by constructing graphs based on the 'rank' and size of places in a given area (Figs. 138–140). It is possible for such a plot to indicate distinct classes of settlement, and thus also focus attention on any marked anomalies.

The Rank-Size Rule

This is a generalisation concerning the size of settlements, based on their ranking in descending order of size beneath the largest city; an empirical observation based on studies of population statistics.

Compact 'Agro-Settlement' – From Village to the Fields

Fig. 136. Lower Kivides, among the hills of southern Cyprus: a compact 'agro-settlement' from which men move out to cultivate the land about them.

Terraces about the village support vegetables, spring pastures among fruit trees, and winter wheat. Vines are grown on the further hillsides, where goats and sheep graze on the rougher parts.

This is a tightly knit rural community; about the church are a few open fronted shops, a café, and houses with outdoor ovens; it is similar in many ways to the other villages about six kilometres equidistant from it—Khalassa, Souni, and Ayios Ambrosios (Fig. 100).

Rural Central Place – Serving Dispersed Homesteads

Fig. 137. Bencubbin in Western Australia: a market town serving the farmers and their families who live in widely dispersed homesteads amid the large wheatfields and sheep paddocks.

The town is viewed from the top of the large grain elevator close to railway (left): this receives wheat brought by trucks direct from the combine harvesters.

This is a service central place for the scattered population, with church, school, hotel, pool, garage, general retail stores and branch suppliers of machine parts, farm equipment, fertilisers, etc. It is equidistant from the four centres of Koorda, Trayning, Mukinbudin, and Beacon, each some forty kilometres away, to the west, south, east and north respectively.

Notice the contrast with Kivides (Fig. 136) where the farmers live together in a close community.

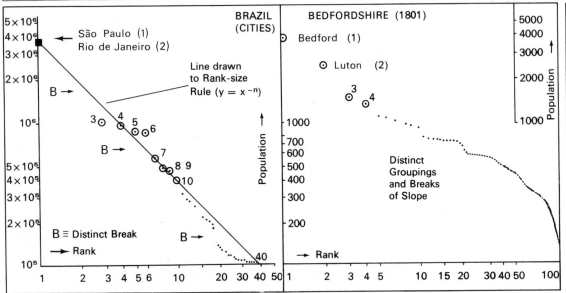

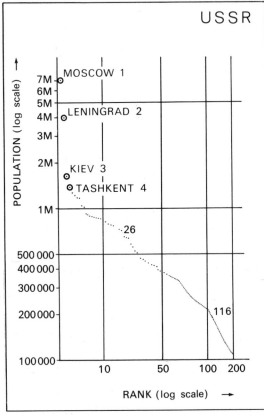

If the settlements in a broad region are ranked in descending order of population size, the population of the nth town may be expressed by the formula

$$P_n \times P_1 (n)^{-1}$$

so that the population of the ninth ranking town (P_9) should be one-ninth that of the largest town (P_1).

Graphs showing the application of this rule to the range of urban settlements within a country seem to show that those countries which conform best have large populations and many long-established, maturely developed, urban centres; conversely, those with a short history of urbanisation and which are predominantly agrarian conform less well. In the latter case the size of the largest city is usually much greater than the rule suggests it should be (the primate city); however, this is also the case in a large number of other countries. It is particularly noticeable that when part of a country is being considered there is often greater discrepancy than in the the whole country. This is what we might expect, for manufacturing districts and towns which are not central market places, may disturb the regional urban hierarchy.

Breaks in Rank-Size Plots

Figs. 138 and 140 show rank-size plots on a national basis; but Fig. 139 shows that of an East Midland county in 1801, then a rural area, with no manufacturing industry, in which one would expect a hierarchical arrangement to show more clearly. There are distinct breaks in slope which could relate to the stepped arrangement of central places described above.

At the lower end of the population distribution scale, as with conditions of primacy at the top, the rule tends to break down. We do not always find more hamlets than villages, nor more isolated farms than hamlets. Here, a detailed field survey is preferable to census figure analysis. The populations of very small settlements fluctuate and cause significant differences in ranking.

Fig. 138. (Brazil[8]). Population of the forty largest cities in Brazil plotted against rank on a log-scale. The position of the 4th, 10th, and 40th cities accord with the rank-size rule; but groups deviate, suggesting breaks between 'orders' of cities.

Fig. 139. (Bedfordshire[9]) Breaks and grouping in the distribution in an English county which retained strong rural characteristics until the mid-19th century.

Fig. 140. (U.S.S.R.[10]) The rank-population plot of the U.S.S.R. (1970) shows Moscow the primate city; marked breaks in slope appear among the top 200 towns.

Location Quotient (L.Q.) for Electrical Engineering (E.E.)

Fig. 141. The Location Quotient provides an Index which shows whether a place or region has more or less than its share of a particular industry. Such figures are useful for regional comparisons, as shown. However, a single factory in a small town may give a high value; while several similar factories in a larger town with more diverse manufacturing may show a lower urban L.Q. for that industry, disguising a more important national contribution.

Since 1801 Bedford, then primarily a county market town (Fig. 138), has acquired other functions, which, as the L.Q. indicates, includes electrical engineering.

$$L.Q. = \frac{\dfrac{\text{Nos employed in EE (in Bedford)}}{\text{Total employed in all industries (in Bedford)}}}{\dfrac{\text{Nos employed in EE (in Great Britain)}}{\text{Total employed in all industries (in Great Britain)}}}$$

$$= \frac{\dfrac{6.1 \times 10^3}{18.8 \times 10^3}}{\dfrac{2.2 \times 10^6}{8.7 \times 10^6}} = 1.3$$

(LQ>1 means a share above the national average)

(1964)   West Midlands 1·2   East Midlands 0·9   (Bedford 1·3)

Manufacturing Towns—Growth and Functions

The ordered arrangement of central places described above involves towns providing services for lesser centres of population in competition with other towns. Now let us look at those towns which are concerned essentially with manufacturing for distribution to areas beyond their immediate region, and often for overseas markets. Such towns, though they may also provide various services for the areas about them, must distort the theoretical patterns.

Certain industries attract other closely related industries (pp. 57 and 108); and industrial clusters, once established, tend to attract still more industry, so the numbers employed in manufacturing may 'snowball'. A manufacturing town may therefore be far bigger than one might expect in relation to other central places in the region.

Basic and Non-Basic Industries

That proportion of the labour force which brings wealth into a town is known as *basic labour*, and their industries as *basic industries*. Non-basic labour provides services for the town as a whole, or produces for local consumption.

As basic industrial employment expands, so the non-basic working population increases. Also, as a generalisation, the larger the town, the higher the proportion of non-basic workers.

The Classification of Urban Functions

We may regard a 'manufacturing town' with many basic industries as an intruder into the theoretical pattern of a hierarchy of central place settlements; but how do we define a 'manufacturing town'? A place offering services may have manufacturing functions as well, yet not be regarded as an industrial manufacturing town, which usually has clearly specialised functions which identify it as a 'textile', 'pottery', or 'steel' town. But, industrial towns are generally multifunctional, and specialist functions often overlap (as within the broad category of 'engineering').

Industrial specialisation may be said to exist when employment in that industry exceeds a 'normal' level: but 'normal' could relate either to the national average of employment in that industry or, perhaps, to the percentage employed in that industry compared with the total employment within the town.

Whatever the figure of demarcation, one town may have employment in, say, textile manufactures just above that 'normal' figure and another well above it—and yet both be regarded as a 'textile town'. In general, when such broad classifications as 'Industrial Town', 'Suburban and Residential', 'Resort', 'Administrative and Commercial Centre' are used, there should be some accompanying statistical and descriptive amplification based on its variety of functions, including social ones, and an indication of population size and composition. A useful guide to specialisation is the 'location quotient' for particular industries (Fig. 141).

Urban Functions

Fig. 142. *Plant treating copper ores at Queenstown in western Tasmania. This has provided basic employment for a large proportion of the town's working population. Sulphurous fumes have long destroyed vegetation on the surrounding hills, whose natural forest was removed by lumbering.*

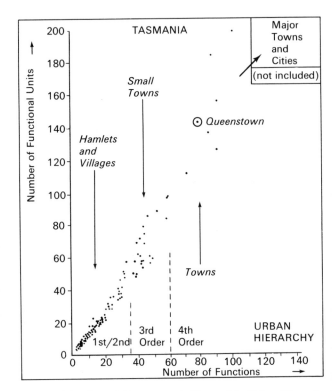

Fig. 143. *The place of Queenstown in Tasmania's Urban Hierarchy (after P. Scott[11]).*

In Tasmania, as elsewhere, the complexity of central places increases with size of population, and the larger places usually have more functions than the smaller ones. Many Tasmanian hamlets have only four functional units, all different—a post office, general store, meeting hall and church. Queenstown, on the other hand, as Fig. 143 shows, has over 140 functional units and more than 80 different functions.

Fig. 144. Queenstown's main shopping centre, showing many of its functions and sources of non-basic employment—retail shops, stores, post office, cafés, garages, etc. Hotels and motels are now much concerned with earnings from the growing numbers of tourists, and thus provide basic employment.

Functions and Urban Hierarchy

We can see that by plotting the number of functional units against the number of functions, as Scott has done for places in Tasmania, it is possible to delineate a whole range of places which fall into a certain class of settlement. Thus Tasmanian central places were found to be in classes of: 191 hamlets (2–6 functions); 171 villages (7–34); 20 minor towns (38–60); 9 towns (72–122); 2 major towns, Burnie (170) and Devonport (199); and 2 cities, Launceston and Hobart (multifunctional) with many special functions not found in other places.

With such information, it is possible to compare the actual urban hierarchy with that in theoretical models based on the rank–size rule (p. 104) and to consider why distortions and irregularities appear. Thus Tasmania's preponderance of lower order centres may be due in part to the broken nature of much of the country; for hamlets predominate especially in areas of extensive sheep raising and in rugged territory.

Queenstown—Functions of a Fourth-Order Place

The first settlement here was in the late nineteenth century when alluvial gold and non-ferrous ores began to be worked in the west. The chief functions were connected with mining, and later with the treatment plant (Fig. 142) which employed most basic workers. Non-basic workers serving other inhabitants in stores, garages, clinics and so on, brought the population to that of a sizeable town, some 5000.

Now, many hotel workers and travel representatives may be classed as basic employees, as more and more holiday-makers visit the beauty of the west and the strange, barren setting of Queenstown itself.

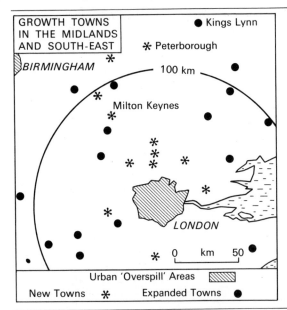

GROWTH TOWNS IN THE MIDLANDS AND SOUTH-EAST

Kings Lynn
Peterborough
BIRMINGHAM
100 km
Milton Keynes
LONDON
0   km   50

Urban 'Overspill' Areas
New Towns *   Expanded Towns

Urban Expansion

Fig. 145. Strict control of the growth of industries and residential areas is particularly necessary in the countryside between the 'overspill' conurbations of London and the West Midlands, and within about 100 km of London itself. Here we see the location of new towns already established, or in the early stages of development. Towns with special schemes drawn up for their planned expansion are also shown.

Fig. 146. Planners have suggested corridors of industrial and residential growth alternating with green wedges of country-side. The growth would take place mainly along the major transport routes, as in the case of Milton Keynes (below).

Others see development in terms of 'growth areas' rather than 'corridors'. 1–5 are likely areas for such planned industrial-residential expansion.

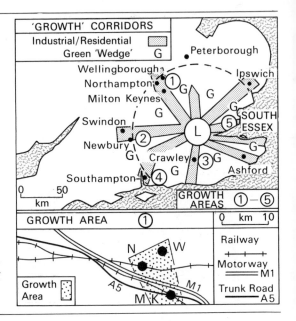

'GROWTH' CORRIDORS
Industrial/Residential
Green 'Wedge'   G
Peterborough
Wellingborough
Northampton   Ipswich
Milton Keynes
Swindon   SOUTH ESSEX
Newbury
Crawley   Ashford
Southampton
GROWTH AREAS ①–⑤

GROWTH AREA ①   0   km   10
N   W   Railway
Motorway
M1
Growth Area   A5   Trunk Road
MK   A5

Growth of Large Urban Areas

From the early nineteenth century, numerous towns developed industrial functions, and greatly increased in size and population. Clusters of urban areas developed, for the industrial towns tended to acquire either specialised activities or else component manufacturing related to their dominant industry. In Britain this occurred in the textile areas on the coal-fields of Yorkshire and Lancashire; there was much regional specialisation among the spinning, weaving, dyeing, and finishing firms. The localisation of ship-building industries on deep-water estuaries close to steel-producing regions also caused a concentration of subsidiary industries, chiefly those connected with marine engineering; along Tyneside, an industrial agglomeration developed, and individual towns became part of a continuous 'conurbation' along the valley.

Conurbations

In some parts of the world historic circumstances and particular economic assets led to concentrations of large industrial towns. America's north-eastern seaboard experienced the rapid nineteenth century growth of population and the trend towards urbanisation; on coastlands settled since early colonial days were favourable industrial sites near deep water and expanding inland markets among the population and industries of the Middle West. This period saw the growth of the great urban centres now embedded in the complex which extends from New England to Washington and beyond, aptly termed a 'megalopolis', of some forty million people.

The term 'conurbation' is generally used where the clustering of industrial centres is followed by the growth of huge continuous urban areas in which towns lose their identity as they merge. This has occurred in Japan in the Tokyo-Yokohama and Kobe-Osaka urban areas, which together include more than twenty million people. On a smaller scale, towns may develop to include former hamlets and villages, which then lose their identity (p. 114).

'Satellite' Growth

In France the growth of administratively independent communes near a city has produced outer rings of expanding satellite towns, which later become attached to the main urban sprawl. Paris has expanded its outer metropolitan urban areas in this way.

Greater London has maintained an outward growth both by filling-in between extending arms of development and by the coalescence of once separate, expanding nuclei. Beyond are more recent, planned, 'satellite' towns, such as Hemel Hempstead; self-contained residential and economic units with many different industries and offices. However, such planned towns are too near the metropolis, and can neither be the answer to growth control nor to London's 'over-spill' problem.

New Urban Development

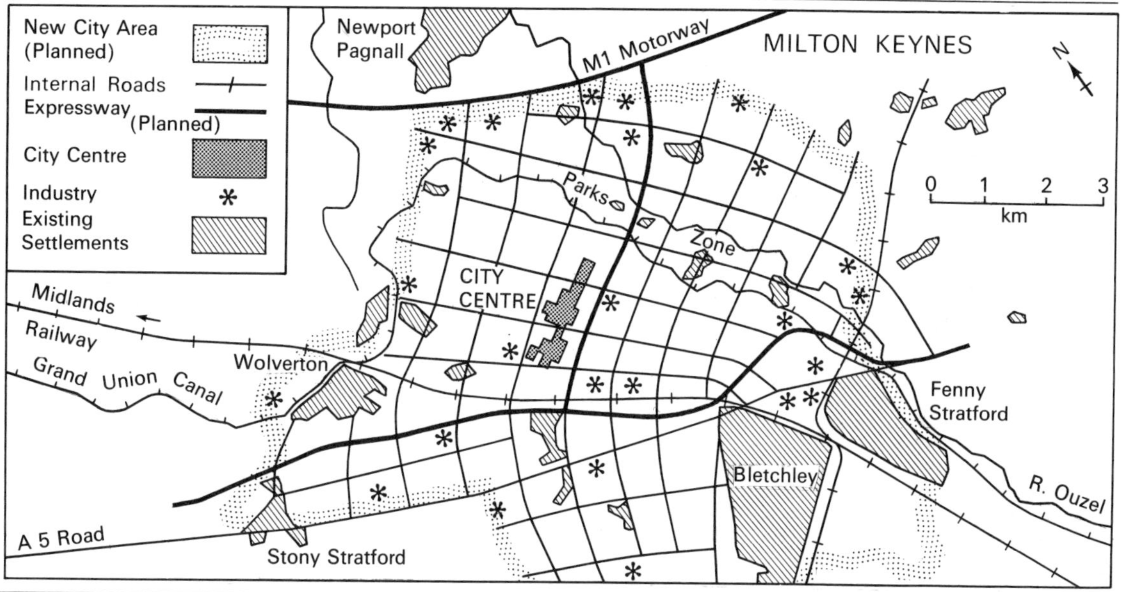

Fig. 147. Milton Keynes, a village near the M1, gives its name to the city which will take in existing Bletchley, Wolverton and Stony Stratford. Development is planned about a one kilometre grid pattern of roads: in the residential area, each kilometre square will contain about 5000 people[12]. A new major route, close to the A5, will be linked by express-way through the city to the M1.

Industry will be largely peripheral. Within the city, the character of existing settlements will be preserved, and the valleys of small rivers used for parks, with artificial lakes. Main shops will be central but with groups of shops and schools local to the new housing estates.

Planned Urban Belts

Green Belts around cities have proved impossible to maintain intact. They tend to be 'leap-frogged' by outer residential areas of an expanding town.

Local remedies, which consider the relationships between a single city and its immediate surroundings, are unlikely to produce an acceptable balance between urban and rural environments. Planning for urban growth should be on a regional or national scale.

Some feel that planning should allow that present cities must merge, and so aim to channel growth along specific belts, aligned with major highways. The purpose would be to leave large, unbroken stretches of rural countryside between these arms of urban growth.

Planning along these lines is behind the creation of the new city of Milton Keynes, which will occupy some 9000 hectares of north Buckinghamshire, and is expected to house a quarter of a million people by the year 2000. It will lie mainly between the M1 motorway and the A5 trunk road (Watling Street), and about the London–Birmingham railway; it closely follows a plan to base new urban development in sectors following main radial communication routes out of London. It includes Wolverton and Bletchley, each with already diversified industries; these, like the other, planned, industrial sites, are to be peripheral to the compact inner residential areas: the latter will incorporate parks and woods, and smaller settlements which will provide elements of individuality.

High-rise urban developments may help to curb lateral expansion; though the creation of multi-storey commercial blocks in urban centres is usually due to the high rental values there. The re-creation of urban areas is considered in Chapter VIII.

The Urban Field

Town and countryside are becoming more and more inter-dependent. Modern transport enables the rural population to use many services centralised in the towns and town employees are able to live in a rural setting while enjoying urban amenities.

The town as a service centre exerts its influence over economic and social groups in an 'urban field' about it. However, fields of influence of neighbouring towns usually interlace. Country residents may go to one town for a certain service and to another for some other purpose; but generally they regard, and use one particular town as their main service centre.

To define the extent of an urban field and the areal influence of a central place, we may select and map various significant indices. We can investigate the catchment area of a town's schools or hospitals, the circulation area of its newspapers, the areas of regular delivery by large retailers, the volumes of movement of forms of transport and their passengers, and study the movement of individuals from the surrounding places into and out of the city. P.113 shows the extent of the catchment area based on the use of central shopping facilities.

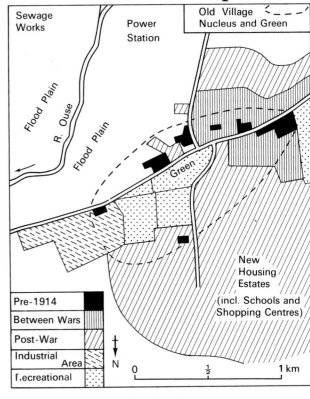

Fig. 149. Phases of development—key to Fig. 148.

Fig. 148. The outward urban spread into the countryside, typified by Bedford's eastward extensions. Sewage works and power station occupy sites near the river (top left). The old centre of Goldington, about the green and near the church, has been engulfed by the modern housing and the industrial estate, which is seen, still being developed, along the Bedford–St. Neots road on the extreme urban fringe. Notice the regular pattern of the new estates, with their local schools and shopping centres.

Fig. 150. Bedfordshire brickworks. At the top left, great grabs are at work stripping the clay to feed the brickworks, whose ovens and chimneys can be seen (bottom left), and are leaving a great scar. Dumping creates delta-like spreads in the old, flooded pits. At the top right, land has already been reclaimed from former workings and new fields created, but a lot of land lies derelict.

The new residential crescents of Stewartby, left, contrast with the old village and farms of Caulcott, right.

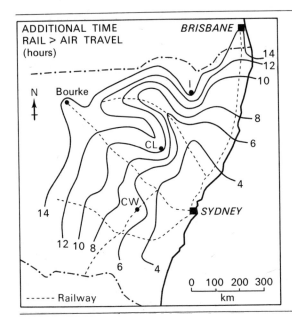

ADDITIONAL TIME
RAIL > AIR TRAVEL
(hours)

BRISBANE

14
12
10

8

6

4

14

12 10 8

6 4

Bourke

I

CL

CW

SYDNEY

0 100 200 300
km

----- Railway

Urban Fields of Influence

Fig. 151. Measurement of time rather than distance allows us to assess the accessibility of places. These isochrones show that Inverell (I), Coolah (CL), and Cowra (CW) are relatively inaccessible from Sydney by land routes; and in fact there is a significantly large flow of air passengers to and from each. (After Quinlan[14])

Fig. 152. The broken line shows a theoretical field of influence of Bedford in comparison with that determined by a shopping survey (Fig. 153). Reilly's Law is used to determine break-points between Bedford and Northampton, Wellingborough, Huntingdon, St. Neots, Cambridge, Stevenage, Luton, Bletchley and Newport Pagnell (using population figures of the early 'sixties—to compare with the time of the survey).

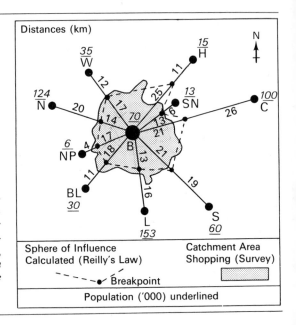

Distances (km)

Sphere of Influence
Calculated (Reilly's Law)

Catchment Area
Shopping (Survey)

----- • Breakpoint

Population ('000) underlined

Accessibility and Urban Influence

The size and shape of an urban field of influence depends a great deal on the accessibility of the centre from outlying places. A realistic way of plotting accessibility involves measurements of time rather than distance.

People living 20–30 km from the centre of a large town may be able to use a fast, through, rail connection or trunk road to reach the urban centre more quickly than suburban dwellers a few kilometres out, who may have to take a circuitous route and perhaps rely on less speedy, or even less regular, forms of transport. With public transport, of course, the interval between vehicles is also significant.

Isochronous maps may be drawn to show equal average times taken for a journey from various points to the city centre, and to indicate the accessibility of functions and services of the urban centre to people living in surrounding areas.

The zone of diminishing influence of the various central functions away from the centre will be different for each function. One group of commodities will have a different area of supply than another, and service areas will be different for different purposes. For instance, the urban field covered by a town's medical services will not necessarily coincide with that of the distribution of the local weekly paper, nor the area served by the local television station. In any event, the limits of an urban field fluctuate. They are also subject to major changes whenever communications or transport are improved.

Influences of Competing Centres

The 'hinterland boundaries' of central places are, therefore, usually broad zones, in which neighbouring centres of comparable size compete.

The outer limits of the retailing services depend to a considerable extent on the size of population of the service centre and its accessibility (seen in the case below in terms of distance).

A theoretical 'break-point', at which the influence of competing centres will be equal, can be stated in terms of the distance along a route between the two. For two centres of equal size, the point is likely to be midway between them: a generalisation based on Reilly's Law of Retail Gravitation[13]. Otherwise the larger centre will have the greater attraction for retail trade, and its trade boundary will be further from it. This may be expressed by the formula:

$$\text{Distance of break-point from A} = \frac{\text{Distance between A and B}}{1 + \sqrt{\dfrac{P_B}{P_A}}}$$

where P_A and P_B are the populations of the competing centres.

This is, of course, a theoretical approach, useful for settlements of the same order, and in a uniform environment. Variations of population distribution between these towns, related perhaps to differences of relief and soil fertility, will be distorting factors.

Catchment Areas

Fig. 153. A survey of shoppers in Bedford's CBD (p. 117), carried out by the County Planning Department[15], showed that within this catchment area the majority of the resident population would normally use Bedford as their shopping centre, and that people of the inner area (broken line boundary) shopped there at least once a week.

The dotted area is likely to be part of the catchment of Milton Keynes by 1981, and of course Northampton and Wellingborough are scheduled for planned expansion.

At the moment Bedford's CBD is a very strong shopping centre for durable goods; for such commodities only London has any real influence on this catchment area, whose residents occasionally visit London for shopping and other purposes.

One settlement may have particular locational advantages enabling it to extend its commercial influence; another may be inward-looking and primarily concerned with meeting the daily shopping needs of its own work force and their dependents, and with distributing specialised products beyond the immediate hinterland; so that the fields of influence of such towns, and their catchment areas for trade, may be far from the theoretical hinterlands derived from figures based on population 'pull'. Nevertheless applications of Reilly's Law may be usefully used in conjunction with population projections to give some idea of changes in catchment areas, as an aid to planning.

Fig. 153 shows the catchment area of Bedford in 1965, based on a sample survey of thousands of households in and beyond this area. It was concluded that, within this, the majority of residents would normally use Bedford as their shopping centre for durable commodities. In the inner area, people would shop in Bedford at least once a week.

Milton Keynes is developing to the south-west, and the likely boundary of its catchment area in 1981 has been calculated and is marked on the map. Such a combination of sampling and theoretical calculation may be used for planning purposes.

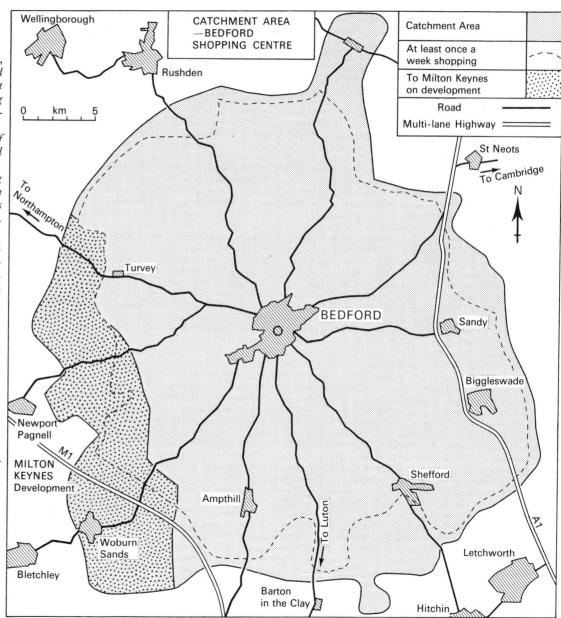

CATCHMENT AREA —BEDFORD SHOPPING CENTRE

| Catchment Area |
| At least once a week shopping |
| To Milton Keynes on development |
| Road |
| Multi-lane Highway |

Fig. 154. *Kempston: within a century, its small hamlets, several kilo-metres from Bedford, have become an Urban District, and the fields which lay beside this central road are now covered by urban development, continuous with the south-western outskirts of the town.*

This is not the outward spread of sector growth, as illustrated in Fig. 157; but, in a sense, a small-scale 'conurbation'—with growth in several directions, but particularly along the axis of the road, resulting in a merging of clusters of population. There is some evidence now of infilling of the hitherto green sectors between this long extension and others growing outwards from the south and west of the town.

As towns expand, planners must decide whether strips, or sectors, of urban growth, with green 'wedges', or radial growth along the whole perimeter, or satellite growth beyond 'green belts', will best preserve a balance between town and country. Evidence of each of these forms of growth is seen in Fig. 164.

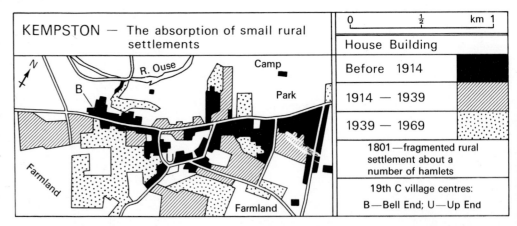

KEMPSTON — The absorption of small rural settlements

House Building	
Before 1914	■
1914 — 1939	▨
1939 — 1969	▨

1801—fragmented rural settlement about a number of hamlets

19th C village centres:
B—Bell End; U—Up End

R. Ouse
Camp
Park
B
Farmland
Farmland

0   ½   km 1

Fig. 155. *Stages in the linking of Kempson and Bedford; and recent expansion.*

Sector Growth

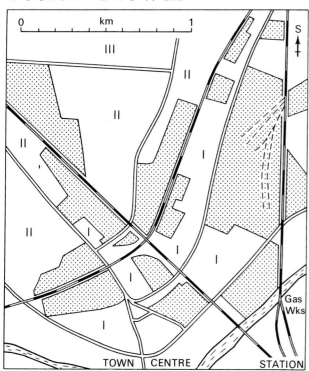

Fig. 156. The shaded areas show the outward extension of industry in a well-defined sector south of the centre of Bedford, away from the railway station and the nearby sites of its early industries. I shows the old industrial-residential districts with terraced housing; II the inter-War residential growth as industry spread outwards; and III the post 1947 housing estates, beyond a new, outer link road. This industrial sector, extending south from the CBD, can be seen in Fig. 164 in relation to the expansion of the town as a whole. Kempston may also be seen to the south-west, now linked to the main urban area.

Fig. 157. Bedford's main industrial sector, between the lines of the railways, south of the river Ouse and the southern extension of the CBD just beyond the town bridge (bottom-centre).

115

Chapter VIII
Urban Structure

Location of Urban Functions

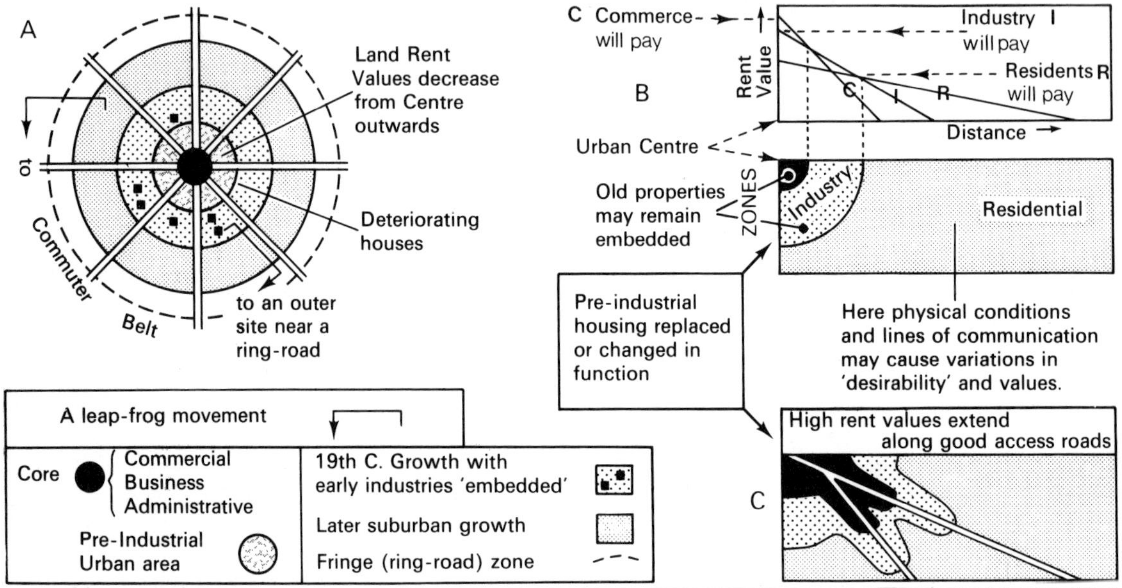

Fig. 158. A shows, diagrammatically, the concentric zones of urban land-use which are found about the centre of towns well-established in a pre-industrial age, and indicates possible outward movements of residents and factories.

B shows, graphically, how commercial, industrial, and residential zoning may develop in response to high central rent values, which, in general, decrease towards the perimeter. In fact, values may vary within the urban area, for some sites are obviously more desirable than others, and, as C shows, sites near good access roads are likely to be suitable for commerce and industry and rent values high.

A

Land Rent Values decrease from Centre outwards

to

Commuter

Belt

to an outer site near a ring-road

Deteriorating houses

C Commerce→ will pay

Industry I will pay

Rent Value

Residents R will pay

B

Distance →

Urban Centre <

Old properties may remain embedded

ZONES

Industry

Residential

Pre-industrial housing replaced or changed in function

Here physical conditions and lines of communication may cause variations in 'desirability' and values.

A leap-frog movement

Core ● Commercial Business Administrative

Pre-Industrial Urban area ○

19th C. Growth with early industries 'embedded'

Later suburban growth

Fringe (ring-road) zone - - -

High rent values extend along good access roads

C

Functions in Distinct Urban Areas

An urban area has many functions spread through the space it occupies. Within it are various flows between the different functional units: flows of people from residential areas to schools and offices; flows of business and communications between factories, hotels, insurance offices and government departments; flows of commodities from commercial units (docks or markets) to manufacturing units (factories); and so on.

In the interests of efficiency many of these functions become segregated, and are deliberately sited in advantageous positions within the urban area. The flow between the units then tends to be channelled rather than random. This creates other patterns within the urban structure: those of vehicle routes to factories, 'bus routes to schools and offices, pipes for water supply and sewage disposal, telephone lines, and many others.

Changing Patterns of Urban Land-Use

The various functional units take up suitable positions relative to one another, to their work force, to potential markets, and to existing communications. Their position is often a response to the cost of occupying particular urban sites.

An advantageous site may become less favourable as the urban population increases and the urban area spreads. With time, the overall pattern may change—though many units, unable, physically, or financially, to move, may become 'historic relics', such as out-of-date workers' houses in a now non-industrial zone.

Congestion in a growing city prevents essential easy access to central commercial and manufacturing sites. If new routes cannot be built, such units may move out to a more suitable location.

Inner housing of the first stages of industrial/urban expansion may deteriorate, and also become cut off from new areas of employment. Some of these dwellings may acquire other functions, or be de-molished and replaced by new high-rise blocks.

Land Values and Zones of Land-Use

Costs, especially land values, are considerations which greatly affect urban land-use. As urban areas have tended to evolve about a central market or commercial core, the need for maximum access to this central area has tended to determine land values and land rents. These are usually highest near the centre and diminish away from it, except where major access routes keep adjacent land values higher than the average for the distance from the centre. But there may, of course, be 'desirable' high-value sites embedded in the outer zones of the urban area.

As land values are high near the centre, one-, two- or three-storey buildings may become uneconomic as dwellings and, as the town expands, be converted to offices or replaced by multi-storey buildings with a larger overall floor space, giving greater financial return.

Urban Models

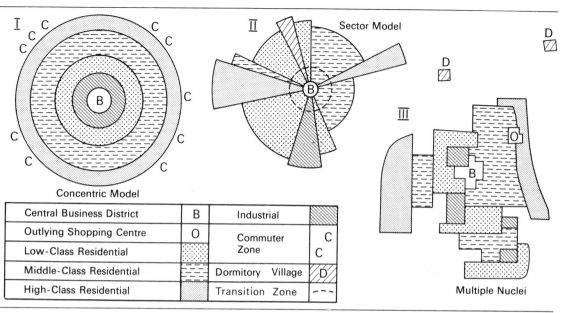

Fig. 159. I is a model of concentric zoning of urban land-use of the kind postulated by Burgess. II shows that many of the older, inner forms of land-use about the CBD tend to retain their relative positions by moving outward in well-defined sectors; though, for instance, the character of the high-class housing in the outer zone is likely to be different from that built in earlier times, closer to the centre. Replacements and changes of function are usual in the area enclosed by the broken line.

III shows development of different forms of land-use about a number of nuclei, and takes into account 'leap-frogging' and the existence of particularly favourable locations for certain activities. What may be most favourable in one age may, of course, be less so in another. Other nuclei, such as parks, schools, and recreational areas, will be located at appropriate places within the town.

Central Business District	B	Industrial	
Outlying Shopping Centre	O	Commuter Zone	C C
Low-Class Residential			
Middle-Class Residential		Dormitory Village	D
High-Class Residential		Transition Zone	- - -

Models of Urban Structure

We can see that there tends to be land-use zoning in a roughly concentric pattern, based on land values. A theoretical model of urban structure, using descriptive terms, rather than rent values, was put forward by an American, E. W. Burgess[16], in 1923. He called the inner urban zone the *'Central Business District'* (CBD), and that immediately about it the *'Zone of Transition'*; beyond the older zone of working-men's houses was a *'Zone of Better Residences'*, and outside the main urban area a *'Commuters' Zone'*.

By and large, we see such a pattern in many towns and cities, but also numerous exceptions and breaks in such regular zoning. The 'Zone of Transition' was seen also as the 'Zone of Deterioration'; but, as we have noted, many former dwellings have become commercial or administrative units; also many industries from inner locations have moved out to less costly sites, often near major ring-roads, and with attendant housing estates (though their head offices may remain centrally located). In some cities, sites or segments have been reserved for industrial development. Thus we may see sectors of development, rather than zones.

A 'sector theory' was put forward by H. S. Hoyt[17]; he suggested that once a sector of a city acquired certain characteristics, residential, commercial, or industrial, they would tend to be maintained as the sector expanded outward with urban growth. Thus high-class residential areas would develop outward from the centre along established routeways, even though inner parts acquired commercial functions.

Again, disruptions are likely, as where leap-frogging by industries from inner areas, and attendant working-class estates, bar the outward growth of a sector; or where nuclei of other functional units become established on particularly advantageous sites. In fact, C. D. Harris and E. L. Ullman[18] published their views of the structure of large urban areas in terms of agglomerations of many different functional clusters, forming nuclei which were established and developing in appropriate locations. Thus, an original route-focus may locate CBD activities; a water-front give rise to dockside functions; financial offices cluster to benefit from close association with one another; component manufacturers set up near a large factory; shopping centres develop in residential districts; and noxious industries be sited on the urban outskirts.

In big cities there are many nuclei, often forming the basis of distinct districts: the CBD itself; light and heavy industrial districts; residential districts; those with medical/dental associations, and so on.

Residential districts generally take up most land. In these there may be divisions on the basis of rental values, access, site and social status.

Other nodal functions may occupy considerable areas, such as University campuses and airports, on the fringe. We should not forget the 'urban fringe', where speculators buy, and farmers do not improve land.

Progressive Replacement in the Heart of a City

Fig. 160. The deep-water docks and the adjacent city centre of Hobart, Tasmania, still have a colonial atmosphere, and many of the old solid freestone administrative buildings, shops, and churches remain.

But, as in all city centres, later structures in steel and concrete replace some of the earlier buildings, and result in such contrasts in style as these—where the old commercial maritime buildings and church, and the ugly five- and six-storey blocks built between the Wars, are dwarfed by recent high-rise developments.

Fig. 161. *Urban contrasts in central Montreal: the old residential houses are on the first of the river terraces which give a stepped urban landscape between Mount Royal and the river, and were once on the outskirts of the main commercial centre of the city, immediately behind the docks.*

Most of the buildings have given way first to large stores and commercial buildings of the inter-War years and then to the recent high-rise developments, which is producing a third generation of central business buildings.

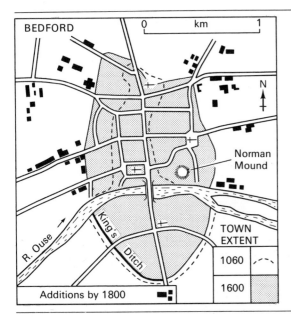

BEDFORD

0 km 1

Norman Mound

TOWN EXTENT

1060	,‑‑‑
1600	

Additions by 1800

R. Ouse

King's Ditch

Urban Growth in the English Midlands

Fig. 162. Bedford's function as a nodal market settlement changed little over the centuries. The broken line encloses known settlement about the ford-bridge site across the Ouse in 1060. The bounds of the King's Ditch is still traceable in the modern road-settlement pattern. The shaded area shows the limits of close settlement in 1600; and at the start of the nineteenth century there were relatively few groups of buildings beyond this.

Fig. 163. The lines of traffic flow and regular movements of people into and out of Bedford. The broken lines show the daily movements of commuters to work, both into and out of the town.

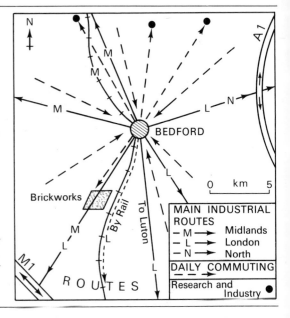

BEDFORD

Brickworks

By Rail

To Luton

MAIN INDUSTRIAL ROUTES
— M → Midlands
— L → London
— N → North

DAILY COMMUTING

Research and Industry

R O U T E S

Zones; Sectors; Nuclei and Reality

We can now observe the structure of two strongly contrasting urban areas with a number of patterns of growth in mind—concentric zoning, sector development, and the multiple nuclei of different functions; none of them exclusive of the others; each may develop in a long-established framework of roads and properties.

Bedford: Its Changing Functions

For centuries Bedford remained a small central place with a regional market, administrative and ecclesiastic functions, and housing a few local crafts and industries. From the time of the Saxon Beda's control of the ford across the river Ouse, it benefited from its focal position. By the eighteenth century it was a route-town noted for the number of its coaching inns. Yet its population and area had grown very slowly since Norman times. It was not until the countrywide increase in population in the late

eighteenth century that there was any notable acceleration. In 1801 it housed only 4000 people.

In 1846 came the first railway connections and soon the beginning of manufacturing industries—iron and steelworks close to the railway. By 1851, there were 12 000 people. But the chief increases in population and residential expansion came when a Charity Act brought a flood of pupils and their families, from outside the town, to its several large schools. Wealthier families occupied new red-brick, slate-tiled housing, developed between the old radial roads from the town centre. The population of surrounding villages was declining, and large numbers moved to the town in the late nineteenth century.

The main railway station was, typically, sited some way from the old centre; nearby, was more industrial development, with many red-brick terrace houses built for the workers. The population nearly doubled in the eighteen-eighties and continued to increase as light engineering and other manufacturing industries came to the town.

During this time the central shopping area, now with prosperous retail stores, was where it had always been—about the ancient market, church square, and High Street running north from the bridge; here, too, were offices of urban and County administration and of the professions.

Between the Wars, the fortunes of the engineering firms fluctuated, and only one really large new factory was built. Electrical and marine engineering were the most important industries, though several thousands were employed in the adjacent brickworks. During this period, the central market, commercial, administrative, and educational functions remained dominant ones. New middle-class housing was spreading in sectors between and along roads to the north-east and south-east of the town, while the rural-urban fringe began to acquire more and more residences of a high social status. The industrial centre had become well established to the south and was shortly to expand (Figs. 156 and 157).

Bedford—Progressive Development

Fig. 164. Bedford: residential and commercial developments in the town and its immediate surroundings.

Concentric zoning, though incomplete, can certainly be detected outward from the CBD: the pre-1914 zone of deterioration and changing functions; the early industrial developments and nearby low-class residential areas; middle-class residential developments (mainly to the north and east); outer high-class residences; and a commuter zone.

Sector development can certainly be seen: in the industrial south (Fig. 156); in the outward extensions of middle-class housing to the north-east; and in successions of high-class residences westwards towards Bromham. While industrial developments on the outskirts and new shopping centres are, like the inner educational establishments (Fig. 168), significant nuclei.

Structure of the Modern Town

Since 1947 the population has increased from 50 000 to some 70 000. Employment has grown at a rate much higher than national rates, with many new manufacturing and service firms employing a large proportion of skilled men. There has also been a marked increase in commuters to London.

Modern Bedford reveals distinct zones and sectors reflecting the cycles of growth. The CBD comprises the old centre, still with a periodic open market, and the High Street; but also an adjacent shopping area with large branch retail shops; this extends westward to where much of the old working-men's terrace housing has been cleared from the inner zone for shopping arcades, central 'bus depot, and multiple car parks. There is some extension of this south of the river, and multi-storey administrative offices now rise up on either side of the Ouse.

Many large Victorian middle-class houses adjacent to the CBD have now become commercial, administrative and professional offices—housing architects, insurance firms, and medical consulting rooms.

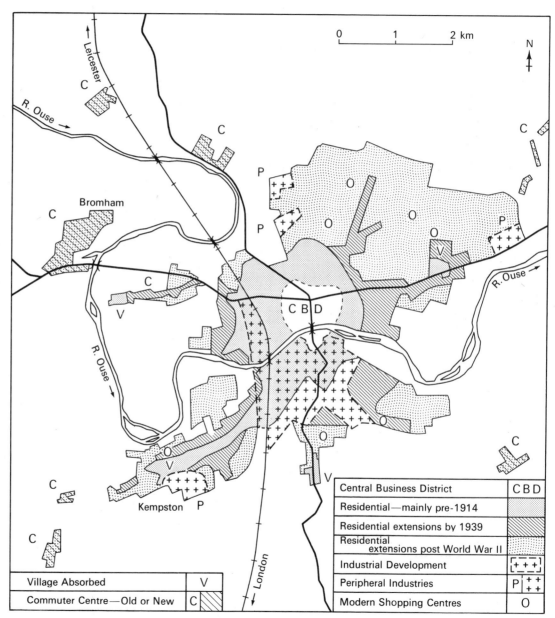

Village Absorbed	V
Commuter Centre—Old or New	C

Central Business District	CBD
Residential—mainly pre-1914	
Residential extensions by 1939	
Residential extensions post World War II	
Industrial Development	+ + +
Peripheral Industries	P + + + +
Modern Shopping Centres	O

Industrial Re-Development and Contrasting Functions

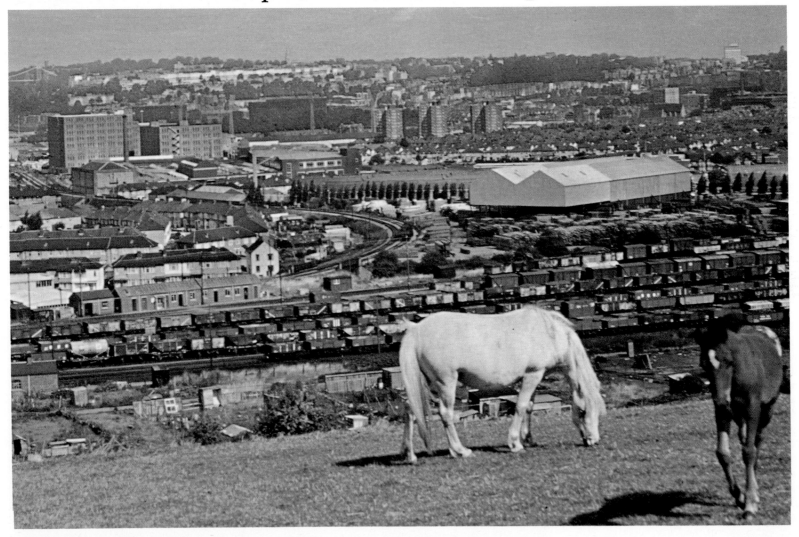

Fig. 165. The rural-urban fringe of Bristol's southern suburbs overlooks an industrial and commercial area between railway sidings and docks, with timber yards, tobacco warehouses, factories, workers' housing, and football floodlights. Clifton's recreational Downs and high-class residences lie above the Avon gorge and suspension bridge (top left). The upper extension of the CBD and University are seen, top right.

Industrial Estates

The industrial areas seen in Figs. 165–7 have contrasting origins and locations; each is still developing, but differs from the planned industrial towns described on p. 109.

Most of the growth in this lower part of Bristol stems from earlier activities close to the docks. As in the past, the main functions are commercial and light industrial. Most of the modern industrial developments are taking place on the outskirts of the city—in particular new industrial estates at Avonmouth, with nearby oil refineries and chemical works, and the aircraft factories at Filton in the northern suburbs.

By contrast, Slough began to develop as an industrial town in the inter-War years. An industrial estate was established there in the 'twenties, clear of the main sprawl of London, and with advantageous sites near the western arterial road and the then Great Western Railway, which, in fact, were followed through the outer western suburbs by an almost continuous succession of factories.

At Slough the growth has continued, and estates now contain light modern industries, including radio and TV, aircraft and automobile parts, plastics, and food products. New industrial growth areas emerge west of it—at Reading and Newbury, along the line of the M4/A4, at Bracknell New Town just to the south, and, beyond these, in the expanding town of Swindon. The map on p. 145 suggests how these westward developments might be channelled; though some favour controlled growth in specified areas, including these ones.

Fig. 166. Part of the industrial concentration at Slough, 30 km west of London. Cooling towers, factories, roads free for industrial transport create a very different industrial landscape to that in Fig. 165.

Fig. 167. Power pylons and cables at Slough symbolise the freedom of industrial estates to be located far from the raw materials of power production and power generators.

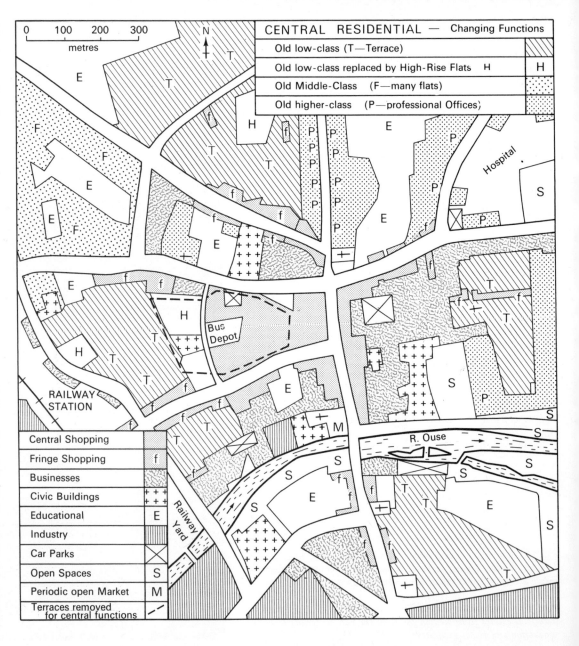

Fig. 168. *Land-Use near the centre of Bedford. Notice :* (i) *the central shopping and business district north of the old bridge ;* (ii) *the 'zone' of small terrace houses adjoining this to the west and south-east ;* (iii) *the extension of the CBD, and a transport depot, created by clearing this old housing ;* (iv) *high-rise flats on clearing in this same zone ; much of the remainder will be progressively cleared ;* (v) *the high proportion of educational establishments, showing a principal local function ; their inner position north of the river reflects expansion in Victorian times ;* (vi) *the high-class family houses close to the centre, but mainly to the north and east ; many have now become surgeries, offices, and small hotels.*

Fig. 164 locates this inner area and shows how the town has expanded beyond it.

CENTRAL RESIDENTIAL — Changing Functions	
Old low-class (T—Terrace)	
Old low-class replaced by High-Rise Flats H	H
Old Middle-Class (F—many flats)	
Old higher-class (P—professional Offices)	

Central Shopping	
Fringe Shopping	f
Businesses	
Civic Buildings	+ + + + + +
Educational	E
Industry	
Car Parks	✕
Open Spaces	S
Periodic open Market	M
Terraces removed for central functions	– –

Bedford—Urban Land-Use

Some parts of the 'zone of deterioration' have become flats, many occupied by immigrant families: the brickworks attracted numerous Irish and Italians, and new industrial growth provided jobs for West Indians, Indians, and Pakistanis. Sectors of this zone have been cleared for multi-storey flats.

There is a well-marked sector of industrial growth south-south-east between the railways. But new industrial estates and electrical component firms have been sited on outer roads, and large new housing estates developed beyond the zones of Victorian housing and the Between-Wars extensions of this.

The local commuter belt has expanded and, with the advent of the two-car family, includes villages far from the town. Some of these villages have housing estates, especially near 'satellite industries' in the country, including electrical, aircraft and chemical research firms. Many research workers and employees commute from Bedford to these establishments (Fig. 163).

Shopping Characteristics

SHOPPING HABITS IN
BEDFORD'S CATCHMENT AREA

Purchased: In Bedford
In District Centres (Locally)
In Other Towns

Fig. 169. Surveys made in Bedford's catchment area in the mid-'sixties showed that most of the shopping for durable goods was in Bedford itself; some patronised shops in 'local' centres beyond the area, like St. Neots and Rushden, or in larger competitive centres, like Luton and Northampton; many occasionally shopped in London.

In these days of rapid public transport, two-car families, and refrigerators, a surprisingly high proportion of food-stuffs are bought during weekly, or bi-weekly, trips to Bedford. Many fruits and vegetables are grown and sold locally, in season. For convenience goods as a whole, there is little shopping in towns other than Bedford.

CBD and Shopping Centres

The relationships between the CBD and the shopping centres in the new estates, in the nearby villages, and in the 'attached' urban district of Kempston (Fig. 154) are changing, and hence of interest to planners.

In the mid-nineteenth century Kempston was still a straggle of hamlets 2–3 km from the town. By the turn of the century it was a nearby Urban District with several thousand people, many of them in small terrace houses, some in spacious Victorian businessmen's mansions. Buildings now link it with the town, and developments have filled in the spaces between the roads of this fragmented settlement; small factories and new estates have been built. Its own cluster of village shops still exist, but on the Bedford road is a new shopping arcade; goods of convenience may be obtained locally, so that journeys to Bedford's CBD can be fewer, though still necessary for many durable commodities.

In Bedford's new estates, planned shopping centres provide many goods of convenience; but interviews have elicited that trips to the CBD were made several times a week because of better selection, and for social contacts.

Urban Surveys

In order to establish many of the facts quoted in the previous pages, it has been necessary to carry out urban surveys. Similar surveys can profitably be organised by student geographers in their own chosen localities, with permission from local authorities. To investigate the rôle of the CBD, for instance, these might include:

(a) Interviews of shoppers over a number of significant days (mid-week or weekends), at particular times, and at selected census points in the CBD—interviewing a random sample, or, say, every tenth woman. One might find where they live, how they travel in, how often they shop there, and for how long, and where they buy selected commodities.
(b) The use of Reilly's Law to suggest a possible shopping catchment area. A questionnaire could be distributed to a sample of households.
(c) A study of 'bus timetables, and road surveys to indicate the volume of traffic on routes to the centre, and its composition (cars, goods vehicles, etc.). The volume and flow of 'bus passengers could be checked, and interviews at various times on selected days would tell of the frequency and purpose of visits.

Urban Land-Use Surveys are best carried out in planned stages, by groups working with existing large-scale base maps, to establish areas used for residence, education, commerce, shopping, industry, industrial storage, parks and open spaces, public buildings, railways and other uses.

Social and residential characteristics are best ascertained by questionnaires distributed on a sample basis in selected parts of the town. The techniques of analysing the data and estimating the accuracy expected by sampling are easily acquired[19].

The CBD and 'Zone of Deterioration'

Those towns in Western Europe which had experienced a rapid growth of population and extensive building about an age-old centre of settlement during the nineteenth century, were considerably handicapped when twentieth century improvements in mechanical transport, industrial organisation, residences, and schools called for much reconstruction. There was a need for new factories, better housing, a more ready flow of traffic, and planned shopping centres to serve modern requirements, with nearby parking spaces.

Some cities, like Coventry and many others in continental north-west Europe, were badly damaged during World War II; so that many of the new ideas related to the CBD, transport mobility, and re-housing could be incorporated in the reconstruction. Others simply had a pre-War legacy of congestion, and inner housing which was in poor condition. Fig. 170 shows this in the Midland town of Bedford; the old terrace housing is indicated by the regular lines and arcs north and west of the CBD.

Bedford was still relatively small, however, and, as can be seen, there was still open farmland surprisingly close to the centre. Much of the new residential growth was therefore created on this open land to the north and north-east, in the form of large estates, with schools and local shopping centres for convenience goods.

The broken lines show the inner clearance which has taken place to provide room for arcaded shopping precincts, a new 'bus depot, and blocks of flats (Fig. 171).

Fig. 170. The centre of Bedford shortly after World War II. The church (C) and the School (S) may be identified in Fig. 170. Some reconstruction, for further education, has begun south of the river.

Fig. 171. Bedford in 1971. The church (C) and school (S), the course of the river and town bridge (right), can be identified also in Fig. 170. In the right foreground is the railway station; older housing remains on much of the adjoining land. The new inner housing and commercial developments are obvious, and, beyond the School (S), housing estates are seen spreading outwards over open countryside (Fig. 170).

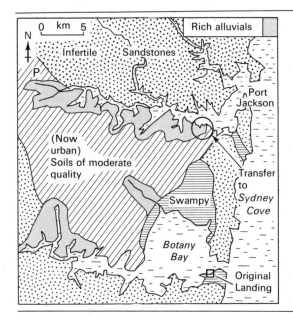

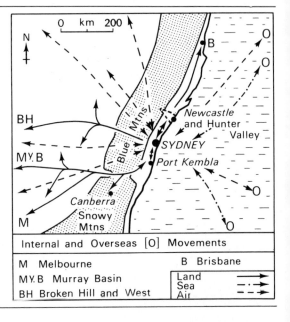

Fig. 172. Soil conditions in the area of metropolitan Sydney as found by early settlers. Settlers were concerned primarily with establishing thriving agricultural settlements. Many soils on the coastal sandstones were infertile, and some alluvials low lying and swampy.

Notice the extent of the deep ria leading to Port Jackson; also the site of the first settlement near Sydney Cove and that of Parramatta, one of the separate inland rural centres making use of richer soils.

Fig. 173. Modern Sydney as a focus of road, rail, sea, and air communications. Despite the few routes through the dissected tablelands in its immediate hinterland, Sydney, like the other mainland State capitals, is a major focus for the movements of people and goods, to and from the other large cities and the rural interior, and through its sea and air ports. The movements are hardly surprising, as well over half the State population lives in its metropolitan area. The location of the harbour and alignment of the lines of communication have always had a great bearing on the city's pattern of development.

Sydney   A Primate City

This large Australian metropolis, lying between the Blue Mountains and the sea, has developed on either side of Port Jackson, split by the drowned valley.

The first European settlement, in 1788, was near one of the southern arms of the ria, Sydney Cove, now at the heart of the metropolis. The sandstones which cap the Blue Mountains and lie beneath much of the coastland form poor soils and tend to restrict agricultural land-use. Separate rural centres were first located on relatively fertile soils further west, with Parramatta at the head of navigable water.

The early industries supplied the isolated colony with its everyday requirements from textile mills, flour mills, factories making agricultural implements, furniture, leather and the like. The subsequent growth of secondary industries and of manufacturing in the metropolis is discussed on p. 132.

Despite the limitations of its immediate hinterland, Sydney, with the advantage of its excellent harbour, became the focus for road and, later, rail routes north and south along the coastland, and eastwards via gaps, to serve the State as a whole. This is understandable, in view of its location between the chief mining areas of a large coalfield, with their metal and heavy manufacturing industries, and its receipt of the primary produce of a huge rural hinterland. It has become a city of size and importance without rival in its State—a primate city.

Most of the early industrial development was on the flatter southern side of the inlet, about the main harbour. But, even before Federation in 1901, the city suburbs had extended eastwards to the ocean, and south towards Botany Bay, and residential suburbs had begun to spread north of the harbour.

Between the Wars, its industrial and residential suburban growth continued, with the northern and southern suburbs linked by the Harbour Bridge; the growth accelerated rapidly after World War II. Parramatta became engulfed in the metropolis, and by the mid-'sixties urban development was continuous for more than thirty kilometres to the southwest and north, and for almost fifty kilometres inland and into the mountains. Most outer residential districts are low density areas, with separate bungalow villas; on the fringe market gardens adjoin land awaiting development.

The Central Business District

The Central Business District (CBD) is located about the site where early settlement began, close to the docks on the southern side of the harbour, where once it was central to the city. Though there has been a large, asymmetric, outward spread, it still lies near the concentrated points of distribution of goods and services—by sea through the wharves, by land through goods stations and road depots.

Transport serving both docks and CBD has to contend with narrow roadways of former periods. Despite new express-ways, central Sydney has problems with rush-hour surges.

Sydney

Fig. 174. Notice the CBD south of the main harbour as the focal point of road and rail communications; the extent to which the city has spread outwards from this centre; and also extensions along the routeways, with an almost continuous urban growth linking once-detached nucleated settlements. Inland, the Nepean-Hawkesbury river runs parallel with, and close to, the edge of the Blue Mountains plateaux. The Green Belt shown here is that designated as part of a planned land-use within Cumberland County (in which Sydney lies) drawn up in the mid-'sixties: it is under pressure in the south, where there is also military reserve land.

The CBD contains modern high-rise buildings for functions which can afford to occupy the central areas with the highest land rents: here are head-offices of firms, insurance companies, development organisations, large hotels, and stores. Decentralisation has taken place in many cases, however, with the growth of large suburban branches of offices and chain stores. Convenience goods in frequent demand, such as groceries, may be purchased in suburban shopping centres; but purchases of many goods with a higher threshold, such as furniture, jewellery, and men's clothing, made less frequently, have been catered for mainly by shops in the central area though many of these items are now stocked in branch stores.

Suburban Shopping Centres

Between the Wars most of the suburban retailing was along the arterial routes, especially near transport nodes, like railway stations and 'bus terminals, and in shopping centres of varying size. Since 1957, dozens of planned shopping centres have been constructed in the suburbs: each with groups of shops, chain stores, branch banks, and with spacious parking facilities catering for people from several kilometres radius. The retailing structure has changed as the older shopping areas have been placed at a disadvantage, though there are still many small neighbourhood shops providing convenience goods.

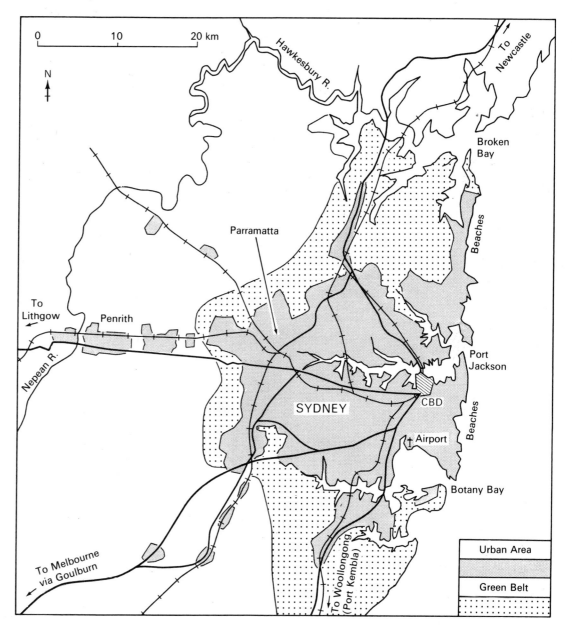

129

CBD, Harbour and Industrial Suburbs

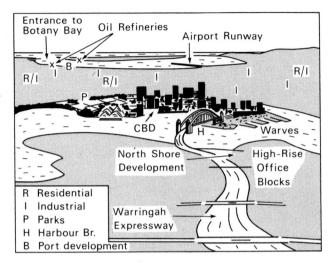

Fig. 176. Key to Fig. 175.

Key labels in Fig. 176:
- Entrance to Botany Bay
- Oil Refineries
- Airport Runway
- R/I
- CBD
- Warves
- North Shore Development
- High-Rise Office Blocks
- Warringah Expressway

- R   Residential
- I   Industrial
- P   Parks
- H   Harbour Br.
- B   Port development

Fig. 175. Looking south over North Sydney to where the Warringah Expressway crosses the Harbour Bridge. The north shore has recently been drastically cleared of old housing for multi-storey offices and residential buildings.

Docks and wharves lie along the southern inlets on either side of the bridge. Behind are the high-rise blocks of the CBD. Beyond this, the inner industrial and residential suburbs stretch away towards Botany Bay where a second deep-water port is planned. Here the airport was built on reclaimed swampland; refineries and chemical industries lie on either side of the Bay, whose southern shores can be seen in the distance.

Fig. 177. Key to Fig. 178.

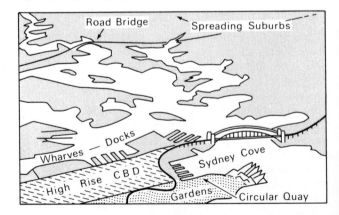

Key labels in Fig. 178:
- Road Bridge
- Spreading Suburbs
- Wharves — Docks
- Sydney Cove
- High Rise CBD
- Gardens
- Circular Quay

Fig. 178. In the foreground, beyond the Botanical Gardens with the new Opera House, is the northern part of Sydney's Central Business District, overlooking Sydney Cove, now in the heart of the city. The expressways can be seen winding through the buildings and over the Harbour Bridge.

The photograph gives a clear picture of the docks and of the inland spread of the suburbs, about the long inlet. Part of the more open, green country beyond the north shore is also visible, along the line of one of the tributaries to the drowned Parramatta river.

131

Industrial Areas

Fig. 179. The three main zones of industrial location within metropolitan Sydney. (1) The older industrial areas, where factories first catered for the needs of the growing population; here there are still textile, clothing, furniture, and food processing industries, but also metals and heavy chemical manufacturers nearer the docks. (2) Much new manufacturing, with particularly strong growth in the south-west: industrial metals are produced in several districts, but the range is wide. (3) Zoning extends to the outer suburbs where factories and estates can grow together; but there are often connections with other firms, materials, offices, and markets nearer the centre.

Manufacturing: Nature and Location

In the early days, and indeed up to World War II, manufacturing was largely dependent on imported raw materials, so that manufacturing industries were located near the docks, wharves, and transport terminals, and close to the CBD. There was an extension southwards towards Botany Bay, where low-lying land was drained for industrial development. Certain noxious chemical industries and tanneries were located on these southern outskirts, and today there are oil refineries and chemical plant around the shores of the Bay. A new deep-water port and industrial complex is planned here, much of it on reclaimed land.

After World War II, manufacturing was less dependent on imported raw materials; but, being dependent on a labour supply, new growth has taken place westward of the centre and in the outer suburbs, where zoned areas were set aside for industrial uses, as part of post-War development planning. Heavy industries, taking up much space near the centre, also tended to react to high land values and many re-located themselves on cheaper land in the outer suburbs.

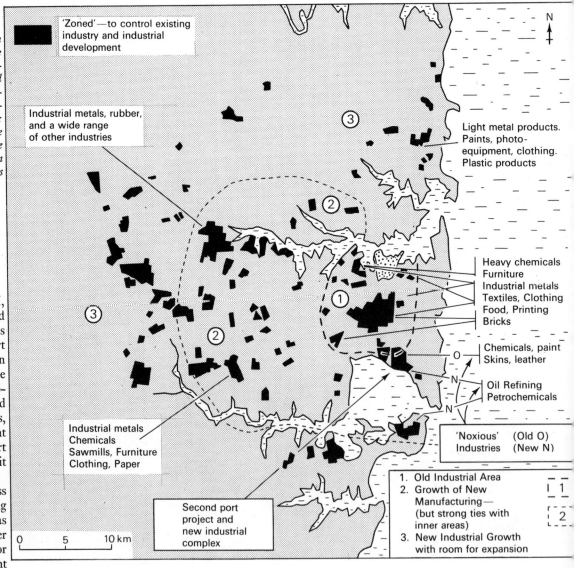

'Zoned'—to control existing industry and industrial development

Industrial metals, rubber, and a wide range of other industries

Light metal products. Paints, photo-equipment, clothing. Plastic products

Heavy chemicals
Furniture
Industrial metals
Textiles, Clothing
Food, Printing
Bricks

Chemicals, paint
Skins, leather

Oil Refining
Petrochemicals

'Noxious' (Old O)
Industries (New N)

Industrial metals
Chemicals
Sawmills, Furniture
Clothing, Paper

Second port project and new industrial complex

0   5   10 km

1. Old Industrial Area
2. Growth of New Manufacturing—(but strong ties with inner areas)
3. New Industrial Growth with room for expansion

Settlement Nuclei

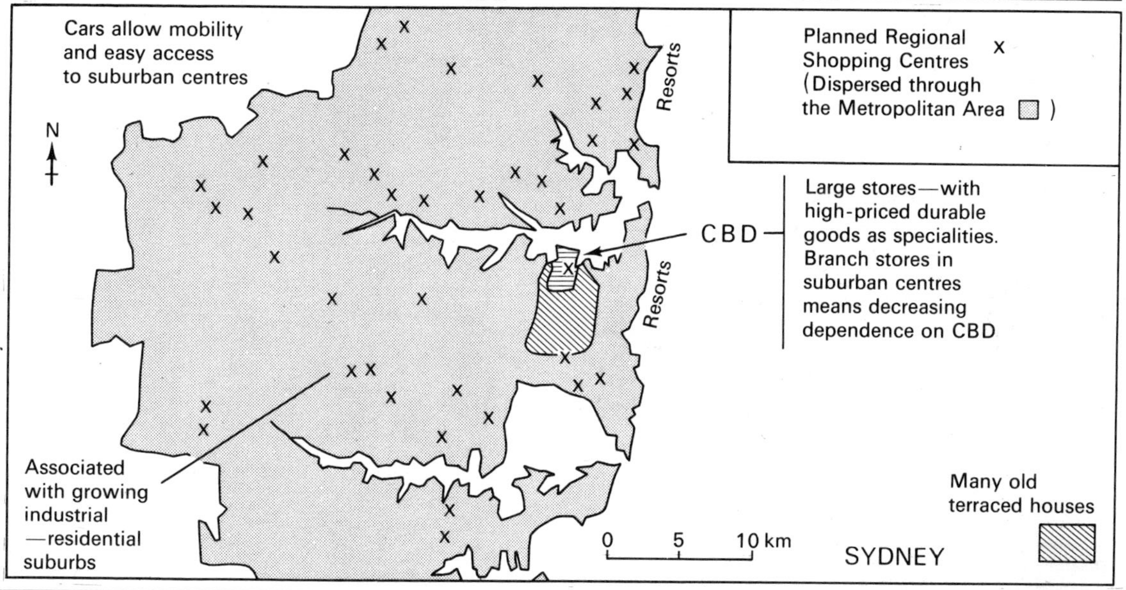

Fig. 180. *As the city sprawls outwards, the growth of planned shopping centres in the suburbs enables people to avoid the main congestion towards the city centre. The whole pattern of retailing has changed in recent times, with some effect on retailers in the CBD; though some central department stores have opened branches in these suburban centres.*

The central part of the city which retains many of the older residential buildings is also shown.

Within the map:

Cars allow mobility and easy access to suburban centres

Planned Regional Shopping Centres (Dispersed through the Metropolitan Area ▨)

Large stores—with high-priced durable goods as specialities. Branch stores in suburban centres means decreasing dependence on CBD

CBD

Resorts

Associated with growing industrial—residential suburbs

Many old terraced houses

0   5   10 km

SYDNEY

Much of the inner land vacated by industry has been acquired by high-rise buildings of wholesale and transport firms, and by other concerns with functions related to the CBD and port areas.

There has been localisation of specific industries within the metropolis. The inner parts have a concentration of the paper and printing, clothing, and food-and-drink groups of industries; though there are heavy chemicals west of this, nearer the docks. To the south are the textile groups, and Botany retains its leather and skin industries; the newer petro-chemicals industries are on either side of the Bay.

The outer zones, to the west, have the most rapidly growing industries, and include industrial-metal processing. Some of the planned industrial areas lie in the northern suburbs, and it is interesting to see that they tend to specialise in high-value products to offset locational disadvantages, mainly due to distance (and time separation) from firms on the southern side of the harbour. They tap labour in these northern suburbs which would otherwise cross to the south for daily work.

Residential Areas

Inner residential areas developed first about the docks; and though much of these has been replaced, first by industrial concerns and now by multi-storey buildings, characteristic streets of the period, red-brick terrace houses with wrought-iron balconies and ornate balustrades, are still embedded in the inner zone. Their fortunes have fluctuated (p. 141).

In fact, the population density is highest in the zone surrounding the CBD and industrial core. There are relatively few permanent inhabitants; but many young couples, and a high proportion of foreign-born, live in the inner suburbs, where there is cheap accommodation and employment nearby.

The intermediate suburbs, which were mainly built before World War II, have a lower density, and a population of higher age; while the outer sub-urbs have a still lower density, except in certain development areas. With recent industrial expansion, the population of the outer zone is increasing rapidly, for there are also many young people in the new suburbs and many recent immigrants. Here there are inter-actions between a potential labour force and new industries. Industries move here, partly because of comparative rent values, partly because the outward population spread attracts industry and commerce.

Post-War planning has aimed at a close relationship between places of work and residence; has encouraged dispersal of both population and employment from the inner areas; the establishment of urban industrial zones 'in a convenient relation to a transport system communicating direct with the city'; and the suburban development of urban communities 'self-contained in shopping and education'. However, some non-conforming industries lie outside these areas, though with restrictions on their expansion.

Residential and Commercial Growth

Fig. 181. This scene, westwards along Port Jackson, typically busy with commercial shipping, shows many of the features of Sydney's modern development. These waterside suburbs, from Rose Bay to Watson's Bay and Vaucluse, near the entrance through the Heads to Port Jackson, have desirable sites of high land value, and high-class residential development. Like other coastal areas, this is really an 'outer' zone (if one thinks in terms of concentric patterns), but truncated by the sea, so that it lies close to the commercial centre (Fig. 184).

The commercial centre itself can be seen to the left of the bridge and the opera house. Opposite are the new office developments on the north shore, where commerce has been slower to develop and there is still little industry.

Inland, a bank of cloud follows the line of the Blue Mountains and gives an indication of the limits of the coastal lowlands.

Harbour-side CBD

Though the CBD is located close to the harbour, where settlement first began, it is no longer central to the mass of the urban area.

Being a waterfront CBD, the concentration of wharves, goods yards, railway depots, and commercial storages, together with the offices, retail stores, and other functional units of the Business District itself, means a great concentration of activities in a small part of the city.

Hence congestion and traffic difficulties have become increasing problems with time. Although Freeway development aids specific points, as do the southern approaches to the Harbour Bridge and the Warringah Highway to the north, there is no freeway system through Sydney comparable with those developed in many American cities. One result we have noted already is a tendency for central retailing to decline, and retailing from suburban branch stores to increase. The CBD contains a high proportion of commercial and financial offices.

Fig. 182. The modern buildings at the heart of the city—the Central Business District of Sydney—seen across Farm Cove, about which lies the Botanical Gardens, which, with Hyde Park provide a recreational function in the city centre.

Fig. 183. Access to the docks and commercial centre is a daily problem in a sprawling city such as Sydney, with its expanding low density suburbs. Many of the main roads in through the suburbs become very congested, and the approaches to the Harbour Bridge, with its toll lanes, must receive and distribute the traffic as freely as possible. Freeways, such as these, make great loops through the centre in order to keep this focal point as clear as possible.

Zones of Urban Development

Central Business District

Light Manufacturing;
Wholesale storage;
Housing deterioration

Heavy as well as light
industries; workers'
housing

Outer residential
areas—tendency for
high income groups
to be far out (and
near coast)

'Rurban' fringe

Mainly late residential
developments north of
the Harbour

Harbour

Resort fringe (- - -)
with own character

In fact disrupted also
by Botany Bay

SIMPLE CONCENTRIC ZONES

Not allowing for: 1 'Pull' of major routeways
2 Effects of urban planning
3 'Leap-trogging' by industries

Fig. 184. A simple model, after Rutherford[20], which shows the usual concentric zoning modified by the special circumstances of configuration and the sequence of settlement (which in turn responded to the physical advantages south of the harbour compared with those of the north).

The normal pattern is disrupted by the harbour and line of the Parramatta river and by the sea. This means that, apart from the functions associated with seaside resorts, there is a narrow 'outer residential' area close to the sea, but also close to the inner city (Fig. 181).

Other factors which will modify this simple arrangement are listed; Fig. 185 gives a more realistic portrayal.

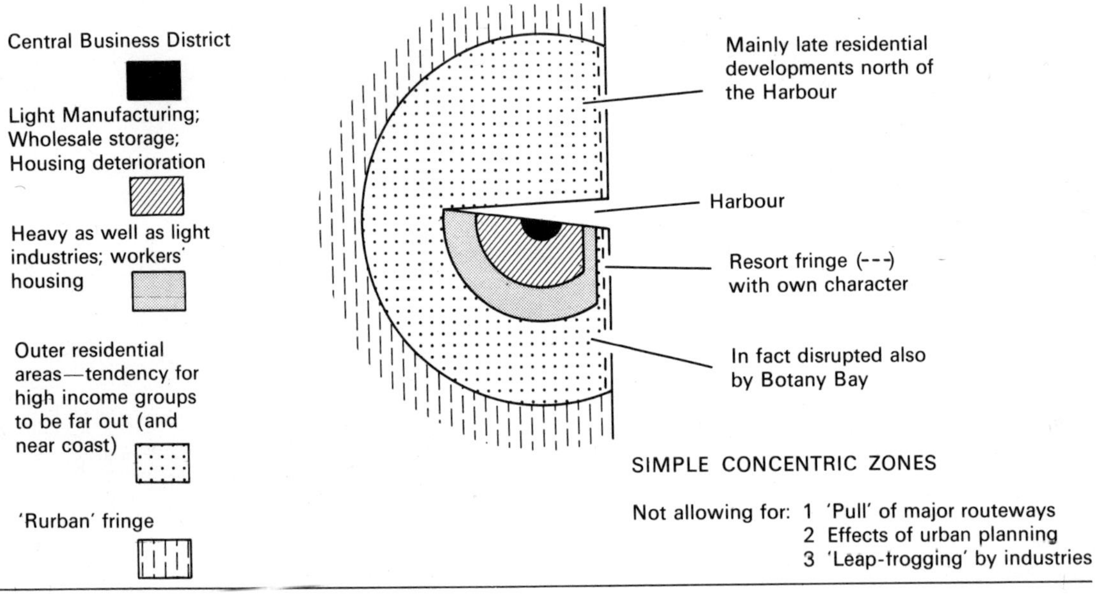

Suburban Housing

Within the broad zoning of inner, middle, and outer residential areas, there are variations in house types, depending on cost and social considerations.

'Desirable residences', highly priced, are found on the extreme outskirts, in the urban extensions into the Blue Mountains, and also along the coast, where particularly attractive sites are available overlooking the entrance to Port Jackson, and on the sandstone cliffs above the many bays and beaches. Even though some of these are located relatively close to the city centre, they really occupy a particular extension of the outer residential zone—seaside.

Physical features have interrupted the zoning and influenced the nature of the residential districts in some areas. Just as the marshes towards Botany Bay influenced the location of early industry and industrial estates, so the deep-set inlets on the northern side of the harbour split up the suburban extensions into separate communities, and into distinct beach areas with their own residential character, shopping centres, and beach amenities. Only relatively recently has population spread onto the spurs between the inlets, and light industries spread over agricultural land, some factories, incidentally supply nearby resorts with fibreglass surfboards and boats.

The Urban Structure Reviewed

We may thus view the structure of this metropolis in terms of zonal patterns of development, disrupted by physical features and by planned land-use areas, some of which are earmarked for industries and others preserved as parks and open spaces.

We may also look at it in terms of sector developments, which are particularly visible along the main western, south-western and north-western routeways; but notice that these are affected by the 'leap-frogging' of former central functions.

We can also take note of multiple nuclei; not only those of industry, docks, parks, airport, etc., but those developed especially as a result of planning policies, and those due to processes of 'conurbation', which have seen Paramatta and other nucleated settlements swallowed up by the metropolitan expansion; we see others created by the growth of the outer shopping centres at focal points in the traffic system, and notice the impetus given to nucleation within the urban area by the new shopping centres.

Structural Models

Local variations of simple concentric zonal patterns have been demonstrated in models devised by J. Rutherford, adapted here as the basis of Figs. 184–5. The distorting effects of the sea and harbour can be seen and Fig. 185 shows the influence of the radial transport routes leading from sectors of inner housing and manufacturing.

Fig. 179 shows the distribution of industrial land within the urban area, and Fig. 180 the location of

Simplification through Models

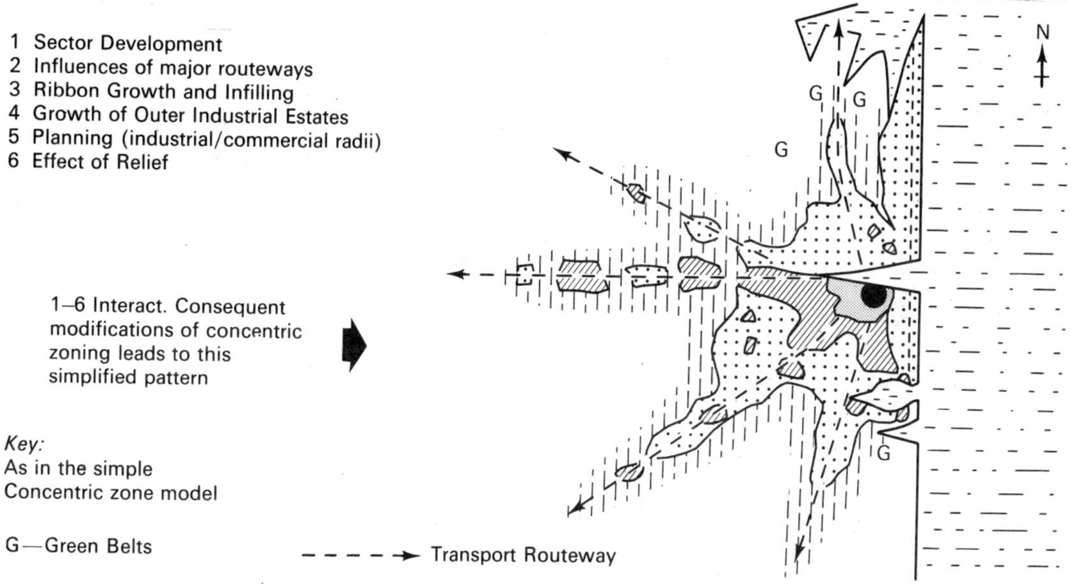

1 Sector Development
2 Influences of major routeways
3 Ribbon Growth and Infilling
4 Growth of Outer Industrial Estates
5 Planning (industrial/commercial radii)
6 Effect of Relief

1–6 Interact. Consequent
modifications of concentric
zoning leads to this
simplified pattern

Fig. 185. A modification of the concentric pattern seen in Fig. 184, showing especially the influences of the major routeways. The actual limits of metropolitan growth are shown (simplified).

Key:
As in the simple
Concentric zone model

G—Green Belts

- - - - ▶ Transport Routeway

Urban Models and Studies of Settlement Patterns

These brief studies of two very different urban areas illustrate that dynamic urban growth may be seen in terms of evolving patterns. As with all complexities of settlement, there is much to be gained from considering these in terms of simplified models; and, again, significant geographical facts may cause deviations from the expected patterns, so that our attention is focused on these causes.

There are, obviously, many similar trends in development within each of these places, town and metropolis; but they show features which are not necessarily typical of other urban areas and are lack- ing in some functions frequently seen in other towns and cities. Sydney and Bedford each contain historic sites, protected open spaces, and other amenities; but, relative to their scale, each seems deficient in well-defined entertainment, exhibition, and recreation centres. In London, Paris and Manhattan such functional areas are easily identifiable, and warrant a sub-division of the inner zone.

We could take many other functions and compare their location within the patterns of development of various cities. University centres, for instance: compare the old University centres in the inner zones of London or New York with the campuses in their outer suburbs, or with the position of newer Universities in the freedom of outer urban zones, as in Kingston, Jamaica, or Swansea, South Wales. In other words, models of settlement patterns may enable us to compare overall distributions and trends in urban areas, and, more specifically, help us to appreciate the comparative locations of individual functions.

the planned shopping centres which have helped to decentralise retail activities, and are of particular necessity in such widespread low-density suburbs.

Settlement Distribution and Individual Movements

The main theme has been 'patterns of settlement', and the emphasis on urban features is surely justified when we consider the high proportion and increasing numbers of mankind now living in complex urban societies. However, the patterns of man's occupation of the land, no matter how dispersed or extensive in character, are visible across the surface of the continents, often remote from the large cities.

But while these *patterns* remain, or slowly evolve, *individuals* are moving in large numbers and temporarily, periodically, or permanently, changing their places of residence. Sometimes their wanderings may change the settlement patterns dramatically, as in the creation of continuous stretches of holiday resorts. Finally, therefore, we look at the nature of such movements and consider some of the causes and results.

137

Urban Functions: Residential/Industrial

The appearance of an urban area varies from district to district, reflecting different functions and also historic periods of growth and development.

Compare these buildings with each other, and with those of pages 134 and 135. They serve different purposes, and also represent changes in architectural ideas and constructional possibilities.

Urban geography can be visually stimulating as well as a socially valuable study.

Fig. 186 (above) *On the eastern edge of the CBD are many of the larger residential houses of the colonial period. Many are now flats or small hotels.*

Here, at King's Cross, close to large modern hotels, is a picturesque group of these houses, which now offer accommodation. In the foreground is a wonderfully vital memorial—El Alamein fountain.

Fig. 187. (below) *New industrial buildings on the outer southern part of the city; part of recent factory development beyond the old industrial area south of the CBD.*

Urban Functions: Commercial/Recreational

The text has mainly considered industrial, commercial and residential functions in towns and cities. Within a large urban area, like Sydney, however, there are sports ovals, race-tracks, cinemas, social clubs, and separate resort areas largely corresponding with the bays.

Recreation is an activity which occupies much time; and people are likely to have more and more time available for leisure pursuits. Planning is as necessary for leisure as for other functions; and again land-use competition and transport facilities are likely to be among the most important considerations.

Fig. 188 (above) *Lorries, carrying wool bales from the interior, arrive at the entrance to the wharves beside Woolloomooloo Bay, in central Sydney. The approach to the docks is often congested and the journey through the extensive suburbs slow.*

Fig. 189 (below) *Deewhy Beach, in the northern suburbs, with its beach-patrol enclosure prominently marked. The recreational advantages of sand and surf so accessible to the main urban area are obviously great; though at week-ends the traffic problems on roads to and from the beaches, and approaching the Harbour Bridge, are familiar ones.*

The Townscape: Survival and Evolution

Fig. 190. A shop in Paddington, about 2 km from the business centre of Sydney. Once the corner grocery shop in a high-class district, it deteriorated with the area as a whole, but is now a smart restaurant in a part of Paddington which is once again fashionable.

Fig. 191. These old middle-class terrace houses of the 1880's, like those in Fig. 190, show the characteristic decoration and wrought-iron work, known locally as 'Paddington lace'. Here we see their location relative to the newer business blocks of central Sydney. As in the old parts of European cities, parking is a problem.

The Suburbs: Residences and Shopping Centres

Fundamental changes in the urban landscape are shown in these facing pages. The character and fortunes of urban areas change with time. This is well illustrated in Paddington. It was once an upper- and middle-class residential area near the heart of the city. Its housing degenerated sadly until the 1960's. Now once again, as with many inner London courts and mews, it has become a fashionable district, conveniently close to the centre for business employees, or for those wishing to live fashionably close to its art galleries, studios, or antique shops, which have taken over many old properties.

In the outer suburbs the picture is different. There are the advantages of life in a more open setting, but now with the added advantage, in many cases, of a conveniently near shopping centre, at any rate by car, without a journey through more congested parts of the city.

Fig. 192. Here are some of the advantages of life in a new suburb, among established eucalypts and planted shrubs; and Fig. 193 shows how some of the disadvantages of decentralisation may be overcome.

Fig. 193. Shopping centres like this, where families can drive in, park, and shop for durables as well as convenience goods, have become a feature of metropolitan Sydney.

Chapter IX
Patterns of Migration

Temporary and Permanent Movements

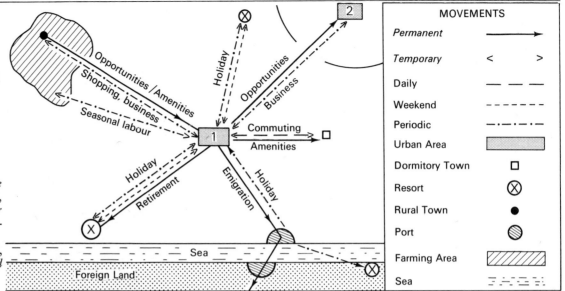

Fig. 194. The population figures of cities tend to give the impression of relatively static communities; whereas, in fact, there are continuous, regular or occasional, temporary or permanent, movements of the inhabitants taking place, involving travel to places beyond the urban limits.

Some of these movements, for labour, business, duty, pleasure, or to a new mode of life, are shown here—related to an urban area (1).

Man's Mobility

We began by considering the movements of people on a semi-nomadic basis, as an introduction to the simpler forms of settlement. In conclusion we consider patterns of human movements under different circumstances, and on different scales of time and distance, but related to existing settlements.

The motives for temporary and permanent migrations are very varied. The causes are often complementary. The lack of opportunity locally, and chances available elsewhere, may cause a permanent movement; an unattractive season at home, and pleasant climatic conditions elsewhere, may cause a temporary holiday movement. There are often more drastic causes of permanent migration: threats to community groups, leading to migration to a more tolerant society in a different environment, for example.

Improvements in forms of transport and communications obviously favour increases in move-ment, both in volume and distance, as the growth of world tourism has shown; people generally have become increasingly mobile.

Temporary Movements

Seasonal migrations such as pastoral nomadism and transhumance are treated on pp. 2–8. They are usually affected by seasonal plant growth, but there may be other commercial incentives. In this seasonal category come the movements of temporary agricultural labour, such as fruit pickers to East Anglia and Kent, where they occupy temporary accommodation during harvest. Similar movements occur in connection with the seasonal salmon fishing on the Fraser river in British Columbia.

Large-scale periodic movements include pilgrimages, organised festivals, and the annual holiday surges to the sea, lakes, or mountains. The economic life of resorts like Brighton, on the English Channel, depends on the arrival of several million visitors each year, as temporary residents. There are mass migrations for shorter periods from cities like Montreal, where week-end movements to residences on lakesides and hills to the north affect the whole pattern of housing, hotels, shops and roads on this southern part of the Shield, empty the city, and jam the roads on Friday evenings.

Such movements involve temporary changes of residence, and are distinct from the daily surges of commuters in and out of urban areas, and to and from the CBD.

Businesses may cause employees to live on sites away from home, or tour abroad for varying periods. These, too, can affect settlement patterns; where temporary townships are built, for instance, such as Cabramurra in Australia's Snowy Mountains, which housed men working on the Water Control Projects; and also where urban districts specialise in commercial hotels for business men.

Scale and Migration

Fig. 195. The percentage of population change due to migration tends to increase with decreasing scale of settlement, as can be seen by considering changes on a world scale and at a local level. One exception being during the early stages of colonisations.

The percentage of those in any particular age group moving in and out of a settled place usually differs from that of other age groups. Migrational changes in Bedford over the period 1951–61, related to various age groups are shown[21]; the degree of mobility is seen to decrease with age, though young people during their middle and upper school years are relatively more static. Opportunities, or otherwise, in various types of employment will, of course, affect the percentages for a particular place over a particular period.

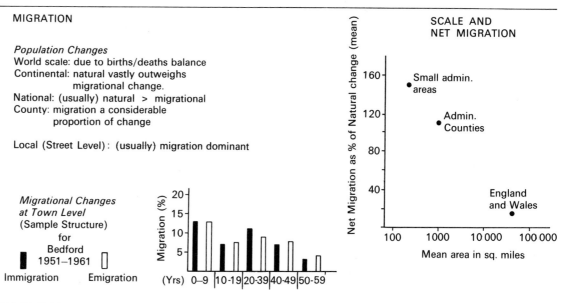

MIGRATION

Population Changes
World scale: due to births/deaths balance
Continental: natural vastly outweighs migrational change.
National: (usually) natural > migrational
County: migration a considerable proportion of change

Local (Street Level): (usually) migration dominant

Migrational Changes at Town Level (Sample Structure) for Bedford 1951–1961
■ Immigration   □ Emigration

SCALE AND NET MIGRATION

Permanent Migrations

Internal: Within a country, people tend to change their permanent residence under the stimulus of specific causes, though waywardness must be involved in many individual movements. Among such causes are: first employment; marriage; subsequent employment opportunities; acquired skills, leading to opportunities elsewhere; shift of employers; promotion to other branches; dismissal, or change in business fortunes; social or racial unrest; inheritance; medical factors; and retirement. This is certainly not a comprehensive list, but focuses the attention on the many compelling reasons for internal movements.

Decisions must be made before moving and selecting a new area to live in, based on such considerations as employment offers, physical environmental attractions, presence of friends or relations, local economic advantages or otherwise (cost of living), and the cost of moving, where the distance factor may be a consideration.

Age, and social and marital status are also factors which make some groups more mobile than others. The young seek jobs, and may adjust more easily; the old may be stimulated to move to 'retirement' areas, or to relatives elsewhere.

Rural-Urban Migrations: The onset of industrialisation and rapid technological developments have usually caused marked movements from rural to urban areas. In England in the mid-nineteenth century there was much depopulation of the less accessible villages, with movements to find employment in the towns. It was only checked by the road and transport improvements of the twentieth century, which has seen repopulation of villages by urban commuters.

Apart from employment opportunities in towns, there are the attractions of shops, schools, and entertainments, which may outweigh such considerations as increased cost-of-living, noise, and pollution.

In some under-developed countries, in South America and India, for example, such migration has led to the growth of shanty settlements and slums; for inward movements have been on a scale which outstrips employment opportunities. In India the movement has tended to be in stages, from village to local town, to regional centre, to large city; always in search of employment.

It is generally in highly urbanised countries that there is now a strong urban-rural flow, mainly, however, to outer commuter zones. In these countries, too, there is apt to be strong inter-urban movement.

Regional Migrations

Some parts of a country may be seen as advantageous from the points of view of opportunities, standards of living, or climatic conditions, so that marked regional migration occurs. This may be seen in the drift to the Midlands and South-East which has occurred in Britain. Here the Birmingham-West

Migration and Living Standards

Fig. 196. The push-pull factors involved in international migrations are related, of course, to conditions in the homeland and overseas, and these vary with time. They also vary in impact on different individuals. Some do not move simply because they are unable to see that the opportunities are there, through lack of publicity, or through their own lack of education or initiative; and for these reasons the very poor, who may be deprived at home, may not seize the chance of a better future overseas.

Opportunities for different classes of immigrant may vary in a country in a relatively short space of time. This is seen in the plots, which show the surge of German farming families and agricultural workers to new lands in the 1880's, and, a generation later, the huge wave of Italian emigration to find work mainly in the new urban areas, which had developed greatly by the early twentieth century. (Statistics by Kosiński[22])

PUSH-PULL FACTORS:
19th CENTURY MIGRATIONS

Push (Home)
19th century population increases
Rural over-population
Competition from the new grainlands
Education and spread of information
—awareness of overseas opportunities

Pull (Overseas)
Abundance of land for development
Developing industries with labour requirements
Transportation improvements
(to, and within, the 'new countries')

Early Waves of Migration
1st Wave: enterprising colonist farmers
2nd Wave: unskilled labour (urban 'ghetto' development)

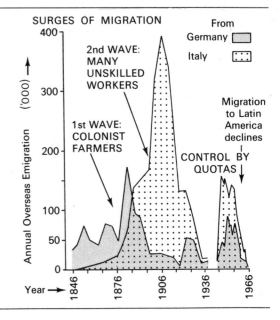

Midlands conurbation, and London and its industrial outer fringes, offer employment in growth industries, and favourable conditions for the establishment of new industrial ventures. The complementary reasons, stressed above, are seen here; for in other parts of the country many of the industries developed before 1900 have seen the demand for their products decline, especially in coalfield locations peripheral to the central-southern expanding industrial zone of the country.

There are often social implications in regional migrations, as seen again in the North-South movements in Britain; also, despite the fact that much attractive countryside lies close to the northern industrial areas, there has been a feeling that the south has climatic advantages, which has tended to make the overcrowding in the south a secondary consideration. The push-pull reactions are strong in this undoubted 'drift to the south', or more accurately to the south and centre, which has continued despite government-sponsored inducements to in-

dustries to move to the 'peripheral' regions and the creation there of industrial estates.

In the USA there have been movements from the South to the North-East and Lakes industrial areas, especially among the black population. There have also been movements from east to west—continuations of the historical westwards migrations of American peoples, especially to California, on the ground of climatic benefits, employment opportunities, and for retirement; as opportunities in the State are now relatively limited, and many of its metropolitan problems are acute, some State authorities have noted, with relief, a falling-off in the volume of westward migration in the late 'sixties.

International Migrations

Here political and economic motives are strong, and contrasts in living standards between countries involved are impelling causes. Population pressures have been the cause of many mass migrations, as

those from the nineteenth-century Ireland and Italy, and from Puerto Rico, to the USA; and recently from south-east Asia and the Caribbean to north-west Europe.

During the main periods of European colonisation, there were movements of colonists to lands where personal hard work and determination could carve out a hopeful future. But, in time, with the continued peopling of these lands and the evolution of strong settlement patterns, there has been less need of immigrants, so that immigration has become selective. Today countries like Canada and Australia really need men with technical skills and capital rather than unskilled labour.

Migration is unlikely to solve problems of overpopulation, especially in countries like India, with densely peopled regions, a high rate of population growth, and low standards of living. Indeed alleviation is hardly possible, for the transference of hundreds of thousands to, say, tropical northern Australia, would make little impression on the hundreds of millions in India, whose population increases *monthly* by numbers of this order.

There has been much successful migration to under-developed lands by people who have capital and technical knowledge, and so can make the most of initially difficult conditions. The Japanese, for instance, have done this remarkably successfully in parts of equatorial Brazil.

Political upheavals have too often caused mass international migrations, with little personal choice involved. This ranges from forced deportations to displacements through invasion or civil war, occurrences of such distressing frequency in recent decades in Europe, Asia, Africa and the Americas alike.

Finally, we come once again to the increasing mobility of man. This is primarily a geography of settlement; but, especially as man is now more mobile than ever, any study of human geography must deal with his movements—to work, to recreation, and in his commercial, political, and social dealings.

References

1 Lösch, A., (translated Woglom, W. H.) *The Economics of Location* (Yale U.P., 1956).
2 Chisholm, M., *Rural Settlement and Land Use* (Hutchinson University Library, 1962), Chap. VI.
3 Christaller, W., (translated C. W. Baskin), *Central Places in Southern Germany* (Prentice Hall, 1966).
4 Thünen, J. H. von, *Der Isolierte Staat in Beziehung auf Landwirtschaft und National-ükonomie* (Hamburg, 1875)—translated Hall, P., (Pergamon, 1966).
5 Coleman, A., 'A Geographical Model for Land Use Analysis', *Geography* Vol 54 (1), 1969.
6 Kansky, K. J., 'Structure of Transport Networks', *University of Chicago Dept. of Geography Research Papers*, (1963), 84.
7 Bunge, W., *Theoretical Geography* (Gleerups, 1962).
8 Brazil, Population of Towns (1967). *Geographical Digest* (Philip 1970).
9 Bedford Statistics (1964), *The Bedford Study—Employment* (County Planning Dept.).
10 U.S.S.R., Population of Towns (1970). *Geographical Digest* (Philip 1971).
11 Scott, P., 'The Hierarchy of Central Places in Tasmania', *Australian Geographer* Vol 99, pp. 131–147 (1964).
12 Brown, E. H., and Salt, J., 'New City on the Oxford Clay', *Geographical Magazine* Vol 51 (11), p. 830 (1969).
13 Reilly, W. J., *The Law of Retail Gravitation* (New York 1931).
14 Quinlan, H. G., 'The Changing Role of Sydney in Australia's Air Transport', *Australian Geographical Studies* Vol 1, No. 1, p. 49 (1963).
15 *The Bedford Study—Central Area: Shopping* (1965) (County Planning Dept.).
16 Burgess, E. W., 'The Growth of a City', *The City*, 47–62 (Chicago 1925).
17 Hoyt, H. S., *The structure and growth of residential neighbourhoods in American cities* (Washington, 1939).
18 Harris, C. D., and Ullman, E. L., 'The nature of cities', *Annals of the American Academy of Political and Social Science*, 242, pp. 7–17.
19 Tidswell, W. V., and Barker, S. M., *Quantitative Methods* (UTP, 1971).
   Toyne, P., and Newby, P. T., *Techniques in Human Geography* (Macmillan, 1971).
20 Rutherford, J., 'Metropolitan Sydney and Economic Growth in Western Communities' *Readings on Urban Growth* Res. Papers 3–7 (Geog. Soc. New South Wales, 1963), pp. 38–69.
21 *The Bedford Study—Population* (County Planning Dept., 1966).
22 Kosiński, L., *Obraz Demograficzny Europy* (Warsaw, 1966), translated *The Population of Europe* (Longman, 1970).

Index

146

Index of Place Names